Lost Treasures
of Arkansas's Waterways

Lost Treasures
of Arkansas's Waterways
Hidden Mines, Buried Fortunes, and Civil War Artifacts

W. C. Jameson

Plum Street Publishers, Inc.
LITTLE ROCK

Copyright © 2015 by W. C. Jameson.
All rights reserved. This book, or parts thereof, may not be reproduced in any form without permission.

Published 2015 by
   Plum Street Publishers, Inc.
   2701 Kavanaugh Boulevard, Suite 202
   Little Rock, Arkansas 72205
   www.plumstreetpublishers.com

Book design by H. K. Stewart

First Edition

Manufactured in the United States of America
10 9 8 7 6 5 4 3 2 1 PB (ISBN 0-978-0-9905971-3-1)

LIBRARY OF CONGRESS CONTROL NUMBER: 2015931891

The paper used in this publication meets the minimum requirements of the American National Standard for Information Sciences—Permanence of Paper for Printed Library Materials, ANSI/NISO Z39.48–1992.

Contents

Introduction 7
1. Lost Mine of the Cossatot 11
2. The Mysterious Silver Bullets 19
3. The Mill Ford Treasure Cave 27
4. Lost Treasure at Happy Bend 35
5. The Lost Louisiana Cache .41
6. The Hermit's Lost Silver Mine .47
7. The Lost Silver of Norristown Mountain 51
8. Turtle Rock Treasure 57
9. Confederate Soldier's Gold 63
10. The Crystal Hill Gold Mine 69
11. The Lost Bear Creek Silver Mine .73
12. The Lost Aztec Mine 77
13. McCord's Lost White River Gold Mine 85
14. Lost Gold Mine in Crawford County 89
15. Lost Silver of Kings River 93
16. Civil War Artifacts at Mud Creek Bottom 101
Selected Bibliography 107

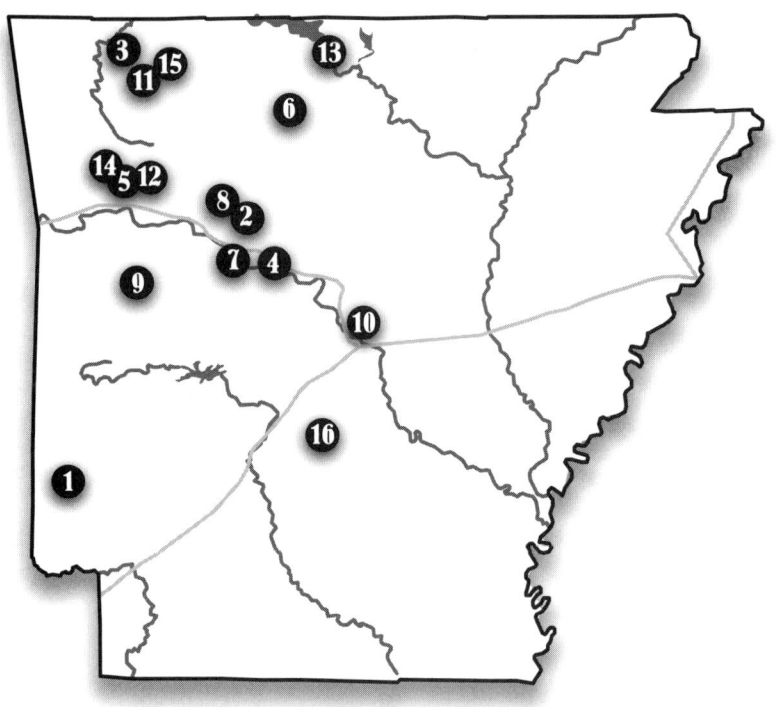

Chapter	Waterway
1. Lost Mine of the Cossatot	Cossatot River
2. The Mysterious Silver Bullets	Moccasin Creek
3. The Mill Ford Treasure Cave	White River
4. Lost Treasure at Happy Bend	Arkansas River and Point Remove Creek
5. The Lost Louisiana Cache	Mulberry River
6. The Hermit's Lost Silver Mine	Tomahawk Creek
7. The Lost Silver Mine of Norristown Mountain	Arkansas River
8. Turtle Rock Treasure	Piney Creek and Moccasin Creek
9. Confederate Soldier's Gold	Brushy Creek
10. The Crystal Hill Gold Mine	Arkansas River
11. The Lost Bear Creek Silver Mine	Bear Creek
12. The Lost Aztec Mine	Mulberry Creek
13. McCord's Lost White River Gold Mine	White River
14. Lost Gold Mine in Crawford County	Hurricane Creek
15. Lost Silver of King's River	King's River
16. Civil War Artifacts at Mud Creek Bottom	Saline River

Introduction

The state of Arkansas possesses a network of waterways akin to the circulation system that courses through the human body, delivering life-giving liquid to large population centers, small communities, villages, farms, wilderness areas, and wildlife refuges. These waterways fill the many lakes found here, providing for water supply, agriculture, and recreation, along with natural and aesthetic balance. Flowing water is an important, vital, resource for The Natural State, and not all of the United States is fortunate to possess the abundance manifested here.

These waterways offer other benefits as well. Arkansas's rivers and streams have long provided food in the form of fish as well as other stream-dwelling wildlife such as frogs, mussels, turtles, and water birds. From the time of the earliest native American inhabitants up to today, people have depended on and reaped the bounty provided by Arkansas's waterways.

As far back as four centuries ago, early explorers used the rivers to breach the frontier they encountered here. They rowed, sailed, and poled up and down the Arkansas River, the White River, the Saline River, the Red River, and other smaller rivers and streams. Where they didn't have the facility to travel by boat, they followed the river valleys overland. Today, major highways and railroads crisscrossing the state continue to follow the same routes.

Waterways have always been important for transportation. The Arkansas River is a major commercial artery, particularly for barges that convey construction materials and drilling equipment upstream from ports as far away as the Gulf of Mexico to Tulsa, Oklahoma, and beyond. Traveling downstream, these same barges may deliver shipments of coal and grain. A number of ports located on the Arkansas River rival some of those found on our oceanic coasts. Thus, Arkansas's waterways factor into a healthy state economy.

Arkansas is rich in other resources, both physical and cultural. The Natural State is a leading producer of rice, soybeans, and other crops. It is also a major center for the harvest and processing of chickens, turkeys, and pigs. Minerals such as bauxite, gold, and silver are or have been mined here. Precious stones such as diamonds and commercial quality quartz have also been harvested in Arkansas.

Culturally, and importantly, Arkansas is rich in history and lore, and so much of both are tied to the state's waterways. Newcomers arrived here in waves—Indian tribes migrating from the eastern U.S., Spanish and French explorers, immigrant groups, and early American settlers. Most often they arrived by following rivers and streams before they stopped to establish settlements, farm the land, and build villages and towns. Traders arrived by many of the same routes. Later, travelers passing through during the Gold Rush toward the perceived Promised Land of California often paused in Arkansas, found something to like, and settled here.

Throughout history, where one finds an intermingling of various and diverse cultures such as emerged in Arkansas, one finds a brisk exchange of stories, folktales, and legends. The Natural State has served as a source for a number of intriguing accounts of ghosts, hauntings, monsters, and lost mines and buried treasures.

It is well documented that early Indian tribes dug silver from the rock for use in making ornaments. History further records that Spanish explorers arrived in Arkansas as early as the sixteenth century in search of gold, silver, and other riches. They found these ores, mined and processed them, and transported them—either to their governmental and church headquarters in Mexico or to Spain to fortify the national treasury.

Early settlers in Arkansas heard the stories of gold and silver mines as well as caches of treasure throughout much of the state. When not tied down with clearing land and operating farms, many of them set out in search of some of these lost mines and buried caches. In many cases, the waterways offered the most obvious and efficient routes to the treasures.

History, geography, culture, legend, and lore—all linked together in an amazing web of interconnecting threads, and all tied to, and in some cases dependent upon, the waterways.

Searching and researching tales of lost mines and buried treasures in Arkansas required a number of expeditions. Long fascinated and entranced by these stories, as well as the promise of locating lost treasure, I journeyed highways, back roads, and trails. I often followed river and stream courses to their sources and camped out in remote hollows and atop steep mountains. I have spent countless hours in libraries poring over archival materials, historical journals, personal diaries, and letters. I have interviewed dozens of people, many of them related to those who searched for—and sometimes found—lost treasures in Arkansas. I met and conversed with men who continue to look for these lost mines and buried treasures, searchers who never tire of the quest.

The treasure is there. It can be found not only in the form of gold and silver ingots and coins buried in the ground or stacked against the wall of an old mine shaft, but in the people and the places one encounters. For the writer, the story itself is a kind of treasure. Some of them, precious gems, were tucked away in the recesses of old libraries or people's memories, sometimes discovered only after diligent and patient searching. The search for and discovery of such gems is no less thrilling than the hunt for a cache of gold ingots. They are there for the taking, and what's more, for the sharing.

1.

Lost Mine of the Cossatot

Dark places, remote hollows, and strange mysteries still occupy portions of southeastern Arkansas's Ouachita Mountains. This region continues to foster tales of ghosts and spirits, bandits and hermits, and lost mines and buried treasure.

The spring-fed Cossatot River originates in and flows out of these mountains. In its upper reaches it is swift and violent, a challenge to kayakers and canoeists. The name comes from an Indian word that means *skull-crusher*. At its lower end, the river meanders, calm and peaceful, transporting a load of fine silt as it winds toward its confluence with the Red River. The Cossatot River is also associated with one of the region's biggest mysteries, one that involves a rich gold mine.

Over time, the Cossatot has relentlessly carved its way down through the overlying layers of sandstone and shale, forming canyons and gorges, shaping the landscape, and providing the unique character associated with the Ouachita Mountains. Here and there, as a result of the removal of portions of sedimentary rock deposits, the underlying granite is exposed. Granite is a dense rock formed during a bygone era when volcanic activity dominated this region. In Sevier County, the Cossatot River eroded away a significant amount of overlying rock—exposing some granite that contains a vein of gold.

This vein was discovered by Spanish explorers under the command of Hernando de Soto, who arrived here centuries ago in search of riches. They mined the gold, digging a vertical shaft that extended well over one hundred feet into the ground. For reasons not completely understood, the Spaniards abandoned the area while the mine was still productive. Some have suggested it was the result of constant Indian attacks; others are convinced they were called back to Spain where their energies were put to use defending their homeland from its numerous enemies. The gold mine was later found by early settlers and then lost again.

During the late 1860s, Dr. Ferdinand Smith drove his family and belongings in a wagon from Frankford, Missouri, to the remote area of Sevier County along the Cossatot River. The few residents here welcomed the physician; up until then, they had no access to a doctor and treated their ailments with folk remedies and potions. Smith became popular in a short time, making himself available to the sick and injured and often accepting payment in livestock and produce.

Dr. Smith had an interest in history, and the people who lived nearby provided information on early settlers as well as the Indians who passed through the area from time to time. In this manner, Smith heard a strange and fascinating tale of a lost gold mine located some distance upstream of his farm on the Cossatot River.

Several years earlier, a trading post had been established at the site known today as Lockesburg, located on the banks of the Cossatot. The post stocked food, tools, clothing, guns, and ammunition, most of which were traded for pelts. The trading post also served as a gathering place for local trappers and hunters.

Once a month, as the prevailing legend goes, a blond, fair-skinned woman, accompanied by four young Indians, arrived at the post, riding a white horse. She wore garments of leather and gold jewelry of rustic make and design. She would purchase foodstuffs and other items, all of which she paid for with gold nuggets. On the few occasions the woman spoke, it was in Spanish. When locals asked how she had come by the gold, she refused to answer. Several attempts were made to follow the woman after her visits to the trading post, but she always managed to elude her trackers.

Now and then, someone would encounter the woman and her companions returning from the trading post along the trail that has since become the old Fort Towson Road. Following one trip to the post, she was seen entering Pig Pen Bottoms, a snake- and wild hog-infested patch of briers and thick brush in the dark woods on the floodplain of the Cossatot River. When the observer told his friends at the post what he had seen, a small expedition was organized to enter the bottoms, hoping to locate the source of the woman's gold.

The party had a difficult time finding a way into the uninviting area of dense vegetation. Once inside, however, they became lost and wandered around for hours, contending with poisonous snakes. Hours later, covered with ticks and chiggers, they made their way out, finally returning to the trading post around midnight—exhausted, scratched, and unsuccessful. The incident apparently put the woman on guard, for she was never seen again.

In time, Dr. Smith purchased a parcel of land south of Rolling Shoals Ford on the Cossatot River. Pig Pen Bottoms was located between the ford and Smith's land. The large thicket appeared impenetrable and resisted all of Smith's attempts to enter it. Undaunted, he hired a group of men to clear the area so it could be placed into production. When most of the tangle of briers and vines had been cut away and burned, the men discovered the entrance to an old mine shaft in an outcropping of rock.

The shaft was nearly vertical. Peering into it, Smith spotted a number of old and rotting timbers that served as bracing. Along with several of his employees, he descended into the steep tunnel only to discover it was half-filled with water. Later, Smith recalled some area history and lore that told of Spanish explorers visiting the region in search of gold and silver. He wondered if this had been one of their mines.

For several years, the shaft remained inaccessible because of the standing water. Dr. Smith and others could only dream of the riches that might lie at the bottom, and at times they spoke of renewing their quest to reach the vein of gold they were convinced would be found at the end of the tunnel. Before his dreams could be realized, Smith passed away.

During the early 1920s, a severe drought struck the area. The Cossatot River dried up to a mere trickle. Wells went dry as the water table throughout that part of Arkansas dropped dramatically. During this time, the water level in the old Spanish mine at Pig Pen Bottoms had receded. A group of men decided to attempt to reach the bottom in search of the gold.

Two men were lowered by ropes into the shaft. Each carried a lantern and a shovel. As they descended into the mine, they noticed rotting timbers all the way down that had once served as mine supports. Clearly, a considerable amount of work had gone into the excavation of this shaft. During his descent, one of the men found a large, heavy hammer lodged between the wall of the tunnel and a timber support. It was later identified as having been cast in the town of Toledo, Spain in the year 1528, thus providing greater evidence of the presence of Spaniards there.

At nearly one hundred feet into the shaft, the two men encountered water and were forced to return to the surface. After two more trips into the mine, the party reluctantly determined that it would be impossible to reach the bottom unless the water could be removed.

In early 1927, another drought struck the region, and the water table was lowered even further. Another group of men—familiar with the tale of the lost gold mine—made plans for a descent. This time they encountered no standing water and reached the bottom at 120 feet. They did, however, find a deep layer of sediment—sand and silt undoubtedly carried into the mine by floodwaters during previous years. Concluding that the fill was too deep to penetrate in order to reach the vein of gold, the men abandoned the project.

Three months later, the region was still under drought, this one far worse than the earlier one. A group of boys who had heard the story of the lost Spanish gold mine decided to make an attempt to reach the bottom of the shaft. After descending 120 feet into the mine, they encountered the deep layer of silt. They decided to dig into it.

For days, the boys labored to remove the sediment, hauling bucketloads of it to the surface at every opportunity. As they carried the fill to the surface and worked their way deeper into the shaft, they noticed that it grew narrower, suggesting they were nearing the vein of gold. By this time they had excavated several tons of dirt. In the process they found more Spanish mining tools, fueling their optimism that a fortune was near at hand.

Then the rain began to fall. The boys were forced to wait out what turned into a deluge, bringing the excavation to a halt. Luck was not with them, however, for the rains did not abate for weeks. In fact, it was the first of a series of thunderstorms that struck most of Arkansas that year, eventually giving rise to the Great Flood of 1927 that placed much of the state under water.

The swollen Cossatot River raged for weeks, the swift waters carrying a heavy burden of sand and silt. It overflowed its banks and spilled onto the floodplain where the mine was located. Pig Pen Bottoms was underwater for days. Area farms were ruined, but residents consoled themselves with the notion that the fresh deposits of silt along the bottomland would result in more fertile soil.

When the rains finally ceased and the floodwaters retreated, the boys went back to Pig Pen Bottoms to evaluate the status of their digging operation. The thick flood deposits concealed the entrance to the shaft.

During successive years, several parties, fueled by the boys' accounts, attempted to excavate the sediment-filled shaft in order to reach the gold. None were successful. Water in the shaft remained an ongoing problem. No sooner would efforts to remove the tons of silt yield some progress than the spring rains would arrive, bringing more floodwaters from the Cossatot. Over the years, the local water table had been rising, filling the hole to within a few feet of the top. All attempts at pumping the water out failed.

Today, the old Spanish gold mine lies undisturbed in Pig Pen Bottoms. Though the renewed growth of briers and brush conceals the location, a few old-timers in the nearby towns of Gillham and Lockesburg claim to know where it is. They have little interest in making another attempt to excavate the shaft. They have seen and heard too much about the difficulties related to the previous attempts. They are also familiar with the unpredictability of the Cossatot River.

Most of them are convinced that a fortune in gold remains at the bottom of the old mine. Some are optimistic that it can be reached using modern methods. Others, however, are certain that no one will ever reach the gold and that the forces of nature and the Cossatot River will conspire to foil their quest as they have done so many times in the past.

2.

The Mysterious Silver Bullets

Beginning in the latter part of the 1860s and continuing well into the twentieth century, thousands of migrants from Alabama, Kentucky, Tennessee, and Virginia journeyed westward in search of opportunities. Many of them wished to leave the war-torn South and begin new lives elsewhere. Others were lured by stories of promise and potential waiting in California and other western states. Some were simply responding to their own sense of adventure. Due to a variety of circumstances, a few of them never got farther than Arkansas and took up residence in the Ozark Mountains.

One such newcomer to the Ozarks was a man named Tobe Inmon. Inmon had grown up in western Kentucky in a family that farmed in a poor, narrow valley in the Appalachians and mostly kept to themselves. Lured by tales of gold that could be found in the American West—coupled with a desire to see what lay beyond the valley—Inmon gathered his wife and two children, packed a few belongings into a wagon, and driving a half-dozen hogs ahead of them, headed west.

After a long and arduous journey that took several months and subjected Inmon and his family to heavy rains, swollen streams, freezing temperatures, and numerous breakdowns, they arrived at Moccasin Creek Valley in Pope County, Arkansas, located along the southern margin of the Ozark Mountains. Inmon came into the little valley by accident: he was lost. He liked what he saw, however, and decided to make an extended camp. The pleasant green valley was narrow and had a stream of cool, clear water running down the middle of it with sufficient floodplain for planting corn and other vegetables. The surrounding oak forest provided abundant timber for a cabin and firewood. What Inmon liked best about the valley, however, was the fact that it was remote. His nearest neighbor lived more than a mile away.

Inmon decided that settling in this isolated yet beautiful place was preferable to more wearisome travel. He went about the tasks of preparing a section of bottomland for crops and constructing a one-room log cabin. At the same time, he built a pen for his hogs and a crib for corn and other harvests. The family carried water for drinking, cooking, and washing in buckets from Moccasin Creek.

The nearest settlement was the town of Dover, twelve miles to the south of Moccasin Creek Valley. Dover was a supply center for residents who lived in the surrounding hills. From time to time, Inmon would haul chickens or a hog into town on his wagon and trade for staples such as flour, sugar, and coffee.

On the rare occasions that citizens of Dover came into contact with Tobe Inmon, they regarded him as shy and a bit odd. Inmon seldom bathed or cut his hair, and his overalls and boots were ragged and falling apart. He rarely spoke to people except to conduct business. He never tarried in town and avoided social contact of any kind. Those few who chanced by Inmon's Moccasin

Creek Valley cabin remarked on the poor conditions in which the family lived. A few stated that the cabin had large open spaces in the chinks between the logs and offered little more shelter than the hog pen.

One day during October of 1903, Inmon drove his wagon into Dover and asked around for a doctor. His youngest son had taken a fever and was unconscious. Normally, the Inmons resisted any help from others, but the situation was desperate. In a short time, he was directed to the office of Dr. Benjamin Martin, the only physician in town. Martin was a good-natured man in his late forties. He was well liked in Dover and during his residence there had delivered most of the children under ten years old.

Martin agreed to follow Inmon out to Moccasin Creek Valley in his own carriage. He remained with the Inmon family for two days and nights while he treated the youngster. At night, he slept at the boy's bedside. In time, the fever broke, and Dr. Martin pronounced the child out of danger.

As the physician was preparing his horse and carriage for the return trip to Dover, Inmon approached him and asked about his fee. Martin, aware of the family's poverty, told Inmon he could settle his account sometime in the future when times got better. Inmon informed the doctor that he did not want to let the bill go unpaid any longer than necessary and presented him with a small canvas sack. Dr. Martin opened the sack and found thirty bullets for a large-caliber rifle. Inmon told him he made them himself from lead dug from an old mine he found "back in the hills and not too far from the cabin."

During this time, bullets were scarce and difficult to obtain. Martin examined these and found them to be well made. Since he was an enthusiastic hunter and sportsman, he accepted them as payment and expressed his gratitude. He packed the bullets into his carriage, thanked Inmon, and returned to Dover.

When he arrived home, Dr. Martin set the pouch of bullets on a shelf in his study. He intended to use them on his next deer hunt, but during the following weeks he became busy treating the sick and delivering babies. As a result, his usual autumn hunt had to be canceled. As time passed, the physician forgot about the little pouch of bullets.

Two years went by before Dr. Martin remembered the bullets. As he was preparing for a deer hunt, he located the pouch Inmon had given him. He placed it on his desk so he would not forget to take it when he left the next morning. That evening as Martin was reading at his desk, he opened the pouch, picked out one of the bullets, and held it in his hand. Taking a break from his reading, he examined it closely, turning it over in his hand. After a few minutes, he began to pick away some of the black residue that had collected in its surface and noticed the lead had a peculiar color.

On a hunch, Dr. Martin postponed his deer hunt and made arrangements to visit Russellville, a larger settlement several miles south of Dover. There, he took the bullets to a friend who was experienced with minerals. To the doctor's astonishment, the friend proclaimed the bullets to be made of almost pure silver. Martin sold the pouch of shells for seventy-two dollars, a handsome sum in those days.

On returning to Dover the following morning, Martin made plans to revisit Moccasin Creek Valley to try to persuade Inmon to show him where the so-called lead mine was located. Early the next morning, the doctor sped along the seldom-used road to the Inmon farm, alongside the peaceful creek decorated with a lush growth of ferns and watercress along its banks. On arriving, however, he found the place deserted; it had apparently been vacant for some time. Driving his carriage to the home of the nearest neighbor, the physician learned that the Inmon family had departed for Texas six month earlier.

During what time remained in the day, Dr. Martin explored around the hills behind the Inmon cabin and wandered through the woods looking for the mine from which Inmon claimed to have dug the metal. He searched until darkness prevented him from continuing and he was forced to return to Dover.

The following morning, Dr. Martin loaded camping gear and provisions into his carriage and drove directly to the Inmon residence again. He set up camp near the creek and spent the next seventeen days searching for the mine to no avail. When he finally ran out of food, he returned to Dover and prepared for another extended stay at the old Inmon farm.

Time and again, Dr. Martin traveled from Dover to Moccasin Creek Valley in search of the source of the silver. Each expedition ended in failure. Weeks and months of searching turned into years, and soon his patients found another doctor to treat them. In time, Martin ran out of money and had to sell his house and what was left of his practice in order to finance his ongoing search for the silver mine. It had become his all-consuming passion, and some thought it had driven him insane.

More years passed, and Dr. Martin—broke and disheartened—moved in with a sister living in Russellville. His health began to deteriorate, and a short time later he died from complications related to pneumonia.

In time, the tale of Tobe Inmon's silver bullets was being related all across the Ozarks. As a result, a number of area residents took up the search. For years, treasure hunters roamed the hills and hollows in the Moccasin Creek Valley area looking for the elusive lost mine. On two different occasions, hunters found ancient excavation tools purported to be of Spanish origin, lending credence to the notion that the early explorers had conducted mining operations in the region. But neither a mine nor silver nor any other kind of ore was found.

Many grew convinced that Tobe Inmon had accidentally discovered a lost Spanish silver mine. Believing it was lead, he used the ore to fashion bullets. Given his poverty, it is ironic that he had great wealth in his grasp but did not recognize it for what it was. And Martin, on learning that the bullets given him by Inmon were silver, wasted the remaining years of his life searching for it.

In August of 1951, a Cherokee Indian named Lawrence Mankiller arrived at Fort Smith, Arkansas, where he sold a large nugget of high-grade silver. When asked, Mankiller stated he found the nugget in an old mine shaft in Moccasin Creek Valley some seventy miles to the east in Pope County. He explained that he had been hunting when it began to rain heavily. Searching about for shelter, he spied the low, narrow opening to a mine shaft and lay down just inside to wait out the storm. While watching the rain fall just a few feet beyond his position, he began poking around in the dirt floor of the shaft and recovered the nugget.

Mankiller was offered several hundred dollars from a group of Fort Smith businessmen to lead them to the old mine shaft. He agreed to meet them the next morning and leave for the location, but Mankiller did not arrive as scheduled and was never seen again.

Piney Page was raised in Moccasin Creek Valley. In the 1960s, he became a popular folklorist and author and often related tales he learned while growing up in the area. Page was convinced Mankiller had stumbled onto the same mine shaft from which Tobe Inmon retrieved the silver ore for making bullets.

Page, in fact, had evidence of the existence of silver in the valley, and he had heard other tales of the precious metal being found nearby. Page once related the story of a relative, Grover Page, who paused while plowing corn in the valley bottoms to take a sip of cool water from Moccasin Creek. As Grover slaked his thirst, he spied an object at the bottom of the stream that appeared different from the rest of the gravel there. On retrieving it, he found that it was a pea-sized nugget of almost pure silver. Following the discovery, several members of the Page family began searching the area around the stream for more silver. Partway up a tributary named Shop Creek, a thin seam of silver and lead was found in some exposed granite. The Page family invested in some mining equipment and proceeded to blast and drill into the rock. Initially, a large amount of silver was harvested, but the seam played out after a few months.

⁂

During the 1970s, an elderly man who lived in Moccasin Creek Valley told visitors that on dark nights during a waning moon, strange lights appeared on the adjacent ridges. These lights, he said, were seen "dancing along the ridge crests." He further explained that Indians always believed that such lights appear over pockets of silver or gold. Some, however, were convinced that the lights signified a curse that had been placed over the area.

In recent years, hunters who frequent the Moccasin Creek Valley during deer season have reported seeing such lights.

Someday, perhaps, the spirits may decide to relinquish their hold on the silver that lies in those hills. Instead of inflicting a curse, they may indeed smile upon the well-intended searcher, perhaps someone like Tobe Inmon, and allow him to find the mine.

3.

The Mill Ford Treasure Cave

In 1825, a company of mounted and armed United States soldiers arrived in an area of the northwest Arkansas Ozark Mountains to facilitate the federally mandated removal of Indian families from their homes. The counties in their charge included Benton, Carroll, and Madison. Once the Indians had packed their belongings into wagons and onto horses and mules, they were escorted out of the area and to locations several days' ride to the west in Indian Territory, now Oklahoma.

The Indians were relatively few in number and consisted mostly of members of the Cherokee, Choctaw, and Osage tribes. The reason for the removal was political and deceitful. Acting out of self-interest, white settlers in the area bombarded local authorities with complaints about the Indians, insisting they represented a threat to hard-working Christian white people.

The truth was that the Indians generally kept to themselves, posed a threat to no one, and diligently worked their farms. The general consensus was that the Indians had the finest, most productive farms and ranches in the region, and that ultimately was the cause of their removal.

Representatives of the newcomers effectively lobbied government authorities to send a military force to remove the natives. The process was orchestrated by Vice President John C. Calhoun, who drafted the treaty and forced the Indians to sign it under penalty of severe punishment. (The eventual "success" of this plan would pave the way for the Indian Removal Act of 1830.) Once the Indians were gone from the area, the white farmers and ranchers made plans to move onto the abandoned parcels of land and take them over.

Other white settlers in the area, many of whom had been long-standing friends with the Indians, saw the removal process for what it was—a poorly disguised attempt by a number of wealthy landowners to procure the newly vacated farms and homesteads.

Several of the white settlers who were friendly to the Indians assisted their neighbors with the move. Entire families arrived from distant locations throughout the mountains to aid in packing and loading belongings and driving livestock to the new land in the West.

When the time to depart arrived, a long caravan of wagons and livestock snaked across the Ozark Mountains toward a location in what would eventually become Oklahoma. The caravan consisted of Indians, their white friends, and the military escort. In time, the forced emigrants and their party arrived at a crossing on the White River called Mill Ford.

The White River carried a significant flow; given the sometimes-swift current, traversing the stream was often dangerous. Mill Ford was one of the few reliable crossings in this region; there were no others for miles in any direction. The ford, located near the present-day boundary of Benton and Carroll counties, is now under several feet of water as a result of the impoundment of Beaver Lake.

As several wagons and a herd of cattle crossed the ford, an elderly Indian watched from horseback some distance away. Seated on a horse next to him was one of the white settlers, a longtime friend of the Indian.

As the last of the cattle entered the river, the Indian pointed to a high limestone bluff near a bend downriver. There, he said, a cave could be found that contained a large treasure hidden by the Spanish many generations earlier. He went on to relate an amazing story.

Years earlier, according to the Indian's ancestors, a large detachment of Spaniards arrived in this part of the mountain range. The detachment was made up of mounted soldiers, escorting a number of ponderous ox carts through the area. Now and then, they were forced to stop and search for a negotiable pass through which they could drive the carts. The legend, according to the old Indian, claimed that the ox carts were filled with silver ingots that had been mined and processed at some location (now believed to be somewhere in present-day Colorado). They were being transported along an unfamiliar route to a river port on the Mississippi, rafted to the Gulf of Mexico, and loaded onto a ship that would carry them to Spain.

Traveling through the Ozark Mountains was difficult. The heavy, ungainly ox carts slowed progress to only a few miles each day. To compound their problems, the Spaniards had arrived in the range during the rainy season. Many of the creeks and rivers were swollen and impossible to cross. The men spent days in wet camps waiting for the floodwaters to recede. The rain turned the already poor trails into quagmires. Time and again, the Spaniards were forced to halt and pull a stranded ox cart from a mud hole or return one to the trail that had slid off. It soon was obvious that the Spaniards were lost. After three days of traveling through hollows and across ridges, they had somehow returned to the location of a previous camp.

The Spaniards and their fortune in silver finally arrived at the White River, a stream it was necessary to cross. After setting up camp, soldiers ranged up and down the river in search of an appropriate crossing. Upon arriving at Mill Ford, the soldiers deemed it satisfactory and returned to the camp to inform the commanding officer.

The next morning, the Spaniards broke camp, hitched the carts to the oxen, mounted up, and headed toward the ford, arriving around noon. During the crossing, they were attacked by a band of Indians that struck with sudden swiftness. The Spaniards, unprepared, suffered heavy casualties during the first volley of arrows and lances. Leaving the ox carts unprotected, they sought shelter among nearby rocks and trees.

Though they fought fiercely, the Spanish were outnumbered. More were killed during several subsequent attacks, and when their number had dwindled to a handful, the Indians overran their position, taking several prisoners. The Spaniards did not have long to live.

The Indians examined the ox carts for useful goods but found only ingots of bright silver. Not knowing what these items were and finding no utility associated with them, they determined that because they were obviously important to the men they had just defeated, others might follow in search of them. The Indians gathered up the ingots, loaded them onto horses, crossed the river, and carried them a short distance downstream to a high limestone bluff. It was this same bluff that the old Indian pointed out to this friend.

Just behind the bluff was a cave known to the Indians. The low, narrow entrance was well hidden among a jumble of rocks and trees, and the cave wound through the limestone rock for a distance of several dozen yards. Into this cave the Indians carried the silver bars and stacked them against one wall not far from the opening. Following this, the entrance was covered with rocks and made to appear much like the rest of the area. The Indians took two of the silver bars back to their village to show the members of the tribe. They kept them for a long time as a reminder of what happened at Mill Ford.

It was sometime during the early part of the nineteenth century that someone identified the bars as silver—and very pure ones at that. At the time, some of the Indians were compelled to return to the limestone bluff, locate the cave, remove the concealing cover, and retrieve the fortune that lay within. The elder members of the tribe, however, cautioned against such things, claiming that to do so would bring bad luck to the tribe.

The old Indian told his friend that many years passed, and save for only a few of the older members of the tribe, the silver in the cave was forgotten. Since the Indians had no use for it and in fact considered it cursed, they left it alone. As far as he knew, he said, the silver is still there.

With the passage of years, the tale of the lost Spanish silver hidden in a cave near Mill Ford was told many times and became part of the local folklore. Many believed it to be a colorful story but nothing more. Then, in 1925, an event occurred that caused area residents to reconsider the tale and take it more seriously.

Two boys were hiking along an old game trail that snaked through the area in which the entrance to the treasure cave was believed to exist. It had been raining for two days and nights, making the trail slick and difficult to negotiate. Tiring of the pelting rain and the muddy, slippery trail, the two boys took shelter under a large tree on a hillside, determined to wait for the storm clouds to pass.

As they sat under the tree with their slickers pulled up over their heads, one of the boys pointed toward two objects gleaming in the distance. At first, they appeared to be rocks, but the shape was unlike anything else on the ground. When the rain subsided, the boys walked over to investigate. The ends sticking up out of the ground were rectangular and clearly man-made. They dug into the muddy dirt and within minutes retrieved two silver ingots, each one weighing, it was estimated, twenty-two pounds.

One week later, the boys carried the ingots to Fayetteville, where they were assayed. The appraiser told them that the two ingots were made from a high grade of silver ore and were very old. Markings on the ingots suggested they were Spanish in origin. Locals familiar with the legend speculated that the Indians had dropped them while transporting them to the cave.

Believing they might have stumbled onto the location of the lost treasure cave they had long heard about, the two boys returned to the area. During the time they were gone, however, the heavy rains of the previous week had eroded away much of the soil from one section of the hillside and deposited it in another. Several trees, including the one under which the boys had taken shelter, had been uprooted and carried down the slope. The topography of the area had been rearranged such that most of it was now unrecognizable. For two days, the boys searched the area for an entrance to a cave but found nothing.

News of the discovery of the two silver ingots soon spread throughout that part of the Ozark Mountains. In a short time, the Mill Ford area of the White River was swarming with treasure hunters. Some attempted sinking shafts from locations at the top of the bluff in an attempt to penetrate the cavern believed to be located underground, but none were successful.

On the face of the bluff overlooking the White River is another cave opening known by locals as Mill Ford Cave. Though it was difficult to reach in years past, some have succeeded in doing so. Many are convinced that this cave is somehow connected to the one that houses the silver ingots. One promising passage does, in fact, lead in that general direction, but it has been closed off as a result of a jumble of rocks from an earlier cave-in.

This rear entrance to the cave—the one located on the bluff adjacent to the White River not far downstream from Mill Ford—is still searched for today. Some insist that the waters of Beaver Lake have covered it, and that entering it may be possible only with special underwater diving gear. At least two searches have been undertaken to try to find the submerged entrance, but both ended in failure. Some claim that a few elderly Indians living in the area today may know where the entrance is, but they have never been identified.

Some also wonder why the Indians have made no attempt over the years to retrieve the treasure for themselves. Some say they continue to believe that the silver represents nothing good, that it is a reminder of a time when intruders violated the peace and harmony of their homeland. They are content to let the ingots remain where they are, hidden deep in a lost cave in the Ozark Mountains near Mill Ford of the White River.

4.

Lost Treasure at Happy Bend

The once-bustling settlement of Happy Bend, Arkansas is little more than a ghost town these days. Nearby farms and a few residences dot the landscape. Cattle graze in the meadows where investors once hoped to locate a prosperous town prior to the Civil War. There is a church here and a cemetery—but little else except faded memories and faded dreams. Fifteen hundred yards north of Happy Bend flows Point Remove Creek as it slowly meanders its way southeastward for several miles before it joins the Arkansas River.

Where the creek enters the Arkansas River, the turbulence creates strong eddies. The French word for eddy is *remu*, and it is believed that the early explorers to the region named this confluence *Pointe Remu*, which was subsequently mispronounced as "Point Remove" by early settlers in the region.

Prior to the Civil War, Happy Bend consisted of a small mercantile center, a blacksmith shop, and the Wilson Hotel. The hotel served as a scheduled stop for the Fort Smith-to-Little Rock stagecoach run, and travelers looked forward to the fire in the hearth and the fine meals prepared by the cook. Businessmen were making plans to open stores in the town. For a time, hopes for the tiny community were high.

After a few months of operation, however, terrible things began to happen in the Wilson Hotel. Years later, once the nature of the horrible events came to light, people moved away and the town withered and died. To this day, according to some, the area that was the setting for the hotel still pulsates with a dark and frightening energy.

Fifteen miles to the southeast of Happy Bend, the town of Lewisburg stood on a bluff above the Arkansas River. At one time, Lewisburg was a thriving community. In the years before the Civil War, it was a prosperous commercial center and for a time served as the Conway County seat. Saloons and gambling houses outnumbered churches here. Livestock rustlers and bandits who ranged the nearby mountains visited Lewisburg often, and robbery and murder were once commonplace.

Into this boisterous environment rode W.O. Wilson one summer afternoon. Little was known about the man, or even what his initials stood for. It was said that he came from Alabama and was chased out of his hometown for stealing from a merchant. For years, Wilson ranged throughout Kansas, Missouri, and Indian Territory, and when he arrived in Lewisburg he brought with him a reputation as a horse thief and murderer. Wilson loved to fight and often challenged two men at a time to take him on barehanded.

Wilson was a stocky man with thick, muscular arms, shoulders, and chest. His thick eyebrows joined above the bridge of his nose, and he wore a full beard. He always donned a black coat with tails and a derby hat, even in the heat of the Arkansas summer.

Not long after arriving in Lewisburg, Wilson bought a parcel of land at Happy Bend. It was located a short distance to the northwest and adjacent to the route followed by the Little Rock–Fort Smith stage run. He wasted little time in constructing a two-story, eight-room hotel. He procured a slave woman to cook and clean and plant flowers by the expansive shaded front porch. In a short time, the hotel gained a fine reputation for its accommodations and food, and travelers looked forward to spending a restful evening there. In spite of his somewhat bullish appearance, Wilson served as the perfect host, often sitting and chatting with guests well into the evening.

After the hotel had been in business for almost a year, odd stories began to circulate regarding travelers who checked in and were never seen again. When confronted by his neighbors about these rumors, Wilson laughed and said the stories were preposterous. He told any and all that he welcomed an inspection of his facility at any time. Nothing was found to suggest Wilson was involved in anything criminal.

For the next few years, Wilson prospered. In fact, people noted, his financial condition appeared to be far above and beyond what one might expect for a small hotel operator. Now and again, another rumor of a vanished hotel guest would surface. Invariably, the sheriff was called to investigate. Nothing was ever found to suggest foul play, but the guest was never seen again.

One evening, a well-known businessman and rancher named Paschal checked into the Wilson Hotel and vanished. As usual, the sheriff was notified, and he arrived at the establishment with a deputy. While the sheriff visited with Wilson, the deputy searched the grounds around the hotel. He was soon approached by two young boys who told him they had found a dead horse in a thicket not far away. The horse was subsequently identified as having belonged to Paschal. It had been tied to a tree and apparently starved to death.

The deputy speculated that Wilson had killed Paschal and hidden the horse in the thicket, intending to return and dispose of it somehow. Constant surveillance by neighbors likely kept him from doing so. Based on this bit of evidence, Wilson and the slave woman were arrested and taken to Lewisburg, where they were placed in a makeshift jail on the second floor of a store. The woman was reluctant to speak to the authorities. While she was being interrogated, she cast fearful glances at Wilson, leading the lawmen to believe she was more afraid of the innkeeper than of the sheriff.

Late on the second evening of his incarceration, Wilson escaped from his jail cell. He crept down to the riverbank, where he stole a small rowboat and fled downstream. Just as he began rowing away from shore he was spotted by a search party whose members immediately opened fire. A second group of men launched another boat and within minutes caught up with the fugitive. They found him lying in the bottom of the stolen rowboat, mortally wounded. By the time the boat was towed back to the landing, Wilson was dead.

When the slave woman was informed the next morning that Wilson had been shot to death, she nearly collapsed with relief. Once she regained her composure, she told the lawmen an amazing story. She said one of the hotel's guestrooms had a secret trapdoor that led to a deep underground cellar. Whenever a guest dined alone, she explained, Wilson would sneak up behind him and club him in the head with a mallet. Then he would force her to help carry the body to the cellar, where the corpse would be relieved of money, jewelry, watch, and anything else of value. Wilson would also knock out any gold teeth and take spurs from their boots. He handed the stolen items to the slave woman, who placed them in an empty flour sack.

This done, Wilson, using a meat cleaver, would dismember the corpse. When the pieces were small enough, he ordered the woman to place them in a weighted burlap sack. Together, the two dragged it across a large field to nearby Point Remove Creek. There, they tossed the bag into the water, where it would sink out of sight. When the sack vanished beneath the waters, Wilson, still clutching the pouch of stolen valuables, would send the woman back to the hotel. When she was out of sight, he would bury it—along with others he had accumulated over the years. Thirty minutes later, she said, Wilson would return to the hotel.

The woman estimated that, during the three years she had been with him, her owner had buried several dozen such flour sacks at a location somewhere between the hotel and the creek. Days later, when the news of the slave woman's confession reached the citizens of Happy Bend, they set fire to the hotel and watched it burn to the ground.

The authorities searched the area between the hotel and the creek for several days in an unsuccessful attempt to find Wilson's buried loot. Modern-day treasure hunters, using state-of-the-art metal detectors, have launched searches but have had no more luck in finding the cache. Over the years, a few period coins and a spur have been found near Point Remove Creek—probably dropped by Wilson or the slave woman—but the treasure cache has eluded all.

The Wilson Hotel has been gone for nearly a century and a half. No one is positive of its original location. It is suspected, however, that the bodies were dumped into Point Remove Creek at a point north of Happy Bend and west of Goose Pond. This is the same place where treasure hunters found the coins and spur.

Today, Happy Bend remains a relatively secluded unincorporated community in southeastern Pope County. Located a short distance north of Interstate 40, it enjoys no direct exits or entrances to that highway. About twenty families live in the area. The only time this tiny community sees much activity is during deer season when hunters arrive in the area.

Researchers have recently learned that the course of Point Remove Creek is somewhat different today than its path during W.O. Wilson's time. With each major flood, the channel was modified. One study suggests that the section of the creek that flows north of Happy Bend may be at least one hundred feet south of the channel it occupied before the Civil War. Furthermore, each flood deposits a new layer of silt on the adjacent floodplain. As a result, Wilson's buried treasure may be deeper in the ground than it was during his time, making it a bit more difficult to locate with metal detectors.

Given recent advancements in detection equipment and ground-penetrating devices, however, it may just be a matter of time before some fortunate treasure hunter locates Wilson's cache. Today, such an accumulation of coins, jewelry, and other items would likely be worth an impressive fortune.

5.

The Lost Louisiana Cache

Near the end of a convoluted route that follows a series of Ozark rivers, creeks, and tributaries lies a long-lost cave that once housed—and still does—a fortune in Spanish gold and artifacts. The existence of this cache is not in doubt, for it was seen and reported during the early 1900s. Since then, the site has been lost and attempts to relocate it have invariably ended in failure. In spite of this, adventurers and treasure hunters journey to the region, all in hopes of finding this cache of immense wealth.

During the mid-1700s, a party of Spaniards transported several burro-loads of gold ingots—along with a large number of golden religious objects—into the Arkansas Ozark Mountains. The origin of this treasure is uncertain, and why and how it came into the possession of the Spaniards is unknown. Some have advanced the notion that the treasure represented loot from a series of robberies in Mexico. Others have suggested that the Spaniards secured gold ingots and artifacts to keep them from being stolen by roving Mexican bandits, then fled the area in search of a suitable faraway place in which to hide the valuables.

Whatever the truth—and it may never be known—the Spaniards reportedly cached the treasure in a small cave located somewhere in the Ozarks in Franklin County. Records of the cache, if they ever existed, were never found, but during the early 1900s, a most interesting and bizarre event occurred in Mexico that led to the location of the gold-filled treasure room, one that involved an Arkansas geologist and petroleum engineer.

During the first decade of the twentieth century, Dr. J. M. Gregory was living in Mexico and employed as a petroleum geologist by the German government. At the time, the Germans were assisting the Mexicans with their oil explorations.

During Dr. Gregory's stay, a delegation from Spain—bearing letters, documents, and maps from the Spanish government—approached the President of Mexico. The letters requested cooperation and assistance in locating and retrieving a large, long-lost treasure in gold ingots and valuable church artifacts. The cache, the Spaniards asserted, had been removed from Mexico and relocated in the United States. The treasure, for reasons no one has ever explained, was referred to as the Lost Louisiana Cache, and the maps indicated it was located in the southern Ozark Mountains. As a result of his familiarity with the area, Dr. Gregory was invited by the president of Mexico to accompany the Spaniards as guide.

The party traveled northward into the United States via train. Once across the border, they purchased horses and mules; the remainder of the journey consisted of long and tedious travel on horseback. On arriving in Arkansas, Dr. Gregory led the group to the small town of Alma, on the Arkansas River, where they lingered for several days to rest.

One week later, they set out eastward along the banks of the river and the next day arrived at the tiny village of Mulberry. At this point, the Mulberry River joined the Arkansas River after flowing out of the Ozarks. The party followed the Mulberry River upstream to Fane Creek, thence to Browder Hollow through which flowed a narrow, shallow stream. They traveled up the hollow until they came to a location in the northern part of what today is Franklin County. Here they set up camp in the shadow of Parker Mountain.

For several days, members of the party, referring to the old maps and documents they brought with them, explored the area in search of pertinent landmarks. One afternoon, a group of searchers arrived in camp and announced they had found the cave containing the treasure, but that it was covered over with rocks that would need to be removed. The Spaniards made plans to travel to the site the next morning, gain access to the cave, and retrieve as much of the treasure as possible.

At dawn the following morning, Gregory was set to accompany the Spaniards to the site when he was informed that he must remain in camp. They explained to him that he was not permitted to know the location of the treasure cache. Disappointed, the geologist set down his pack. Once the group was out of sight, however, he followed at a distance. A short time later he found himself near the top of a prominence called The Summit, located just to the northwest of Parker Mountain. Gregory saw the Spaniards gathered near the base of a limestone cliff less than a hundred feet below. He crept to a location behind a large rock, where he hid and watched the activities from a distance.

Staying out of sight, the geologist watched as the Spaniards moved rocks and debris and exposed the entrance to a cave. Once cleared, two men stood outside the opening while the rest entered.

Moments later, several men exited the cave, each one carrying a gold ingot or a golden religious object. More men followed, and Gregory watched as they brought out more ingots, crosses, chalices, and scepters. Two Spaniards struggled with what appeared to be a heavy pot, about eighteen inches tall and ten inches in diameter by Gregory's estimate. The pot appeared to be made of gold and decorated with large diamonds. From his place of concealment, he estimated each was at least two carats in size.

As Gregory hid behind the rocks, he watched for the remainder of the day as the Spaniards carried out more than one hundred items. As the day wore on, the geologist, who had neglected to pack water and food, grew hungry and thirsty. Undetected, he slipped away and returned to the campsite.

That evening, when the Spaniards arrived back at the camp, they carried the treasure they had removed from the cave and stacked it up at a central location. Pointing to the stack, one of them explained to Gregory that is was the result of only the first trip into the cave; there was much more treasure still to be to recovered. As the days passed, more ingots and objects were recovered, and the pile of golden items grew to be as tall as a man.

Years later, when interviewed, Gregory said the Spaniards spent almost two months at the camp near Parker Mountain. He estimated that during that time they had removed millions of dollars' worth of gold ingots and objects from the cave. It became obvious to Gregory that the amount of treasure that had been cached was immense. At one point during their stay in camp, three of the men were sent off to procure more mules to assist in transporting the fortune.

The day came when it was time to return to Mexico. With the treasure loaded onto twelve mules and several spare horses, the Spaniards abandoned the camp and set out toward the south,

Gregory riding with them. During the days of travel, Gregory entered into conversation with some of the Spaniards, who told him that the treasure would be eventually transported back to Spain. Following that, an expedition would return to the cave and retrieve more of the treasure. When Gregory asked how much of the treasure was left behind, one of the Spaniards told him "almost three times as much as we have removed."

After reaching the prescribed destination in Mexico, the Spaniards made arrangements to escort the treasure to the East Coast, where it would be loaded onto a ship and transported back to Spain. Before departing, the Spaniards paid Gregory handsomely for his services and told him they would contact him again should they ever return. Before leaving, he learned from one of the Spaniards that, due to certain political and logistical problems, a return trip to retrieve more of the treasure was not imminent. Gregory returned to his job as a petroleum engineer.

For months, Gregory contemplated resigning from his position, returning to Arkansas, and retrieving some of the treasure from the cave near Parker Mountain for himself. He was concerned, however, that if any of the treasure was found missing that he would be suspected by the Spaniards of stealing it. He decided to wait for a while. Years passed, and as far as he knew, the Spaniards never returned to claim more of the treasure. Gregory was content with his job with the Germans and was well paid. He was able to provide a good life for himself and his family. Still, he thought often about the huge cache of treasure hidden away in a remote portion of the Ozarks.

When 1920 arrived, Gregory's work with the Germans was finished and he made plans to return to the United States. In time, he settled in Little Rock, where he remained busy with family and his consulting business. All that time, however, his thoughts seldom strayed from the great fortune he knew was awaiting retrieval in the remote cave in the Ozark Mountains.

Gregory grew old and infirm before he was able to travel to the Ozarks to recover any of the Lost Louisiana Cache. With his contacts in Mexico, he tried to keep apprised of the return of the Spaniards and a subsequent trip to the Parker Mountain area to recover more of the treasure; according to his informants, however, they never returned.

Dr. Gregory passed away before realizing his dream of recovering some of the Spanish treasure. As far as is known, he left no map or directions to the cache. All he ever related to anyone was that it was necessary to follow the Mulberry River to one of its tributaries called Fane Creek, then on to another stream that flowed through Browder Hollow. The treasure cave was located not far from the upper reaches of the hollow and "near the top of The Summit near Parker Mountain in Franklin County."

As far as anyone knows, the treasure is still there.

6.

The Hermit's Lost Silver Mine

In the few years before and after the Civil War, a hermit lived deep in the woods and mountains not far from the town of St. Joe in Searcy County. Area residents knew him only as Old Man Tabor, and the elderly gent would arrive in town on foot two or three times a month to purchase coffee, flour, bacon, and sugar. That in itself was not unusual, for several other old-timers did the same thing. What distinguished Old Man Tabor from the others is that he always paid with silver ore.

Invariably, Tabor was asked by the owner of the mercantile about the origin of his silver, and the hermit always responded with a toothless cackle, breaking into a strange and awkward dance around the store and in a singsong manner taunting any and all within earshot that no one would ever be able to find his mine. On several occasions, townsmen tried to follow Tabor when he left St. Joe and headed for his shack near Tomahawk Creek, but the old man always managed to elude them.

It was Tabor's habit to come to town a few days before Christmas each year. In addition to his normal supplies, he always treated himself to a bag of hard candy. Christmas of 1865 came and went, but no one had seen Tabor. Since he was quite elderly, the locals assumed that the old man had finally met his death somewhere deep in the mountains. He was never seen again.

Now and then, someone would venture into the hills and forests near Tomahawk Creek in search of the old hermit's mine, but no one ever found it. People searched off and on for fifty years, but in time the story of Old Man Tabor and his secret silver mine was forgotten.

During the 1920s, a family named Taylor owned a parcel of land along Tomahawk Creek. They built a cabin and grew corn and hay where the bottomland was suitable. In addition, they managed to raise a healthy herd of cattle. All in all they earned a decent living from their labors. One morning in 1924, Hulcie Taylor took his youngest daughter with him to search for some cows that had strayed from the herd. Finding the tracks of the errant cattle, they followed them along a stretch of Tomahawk Creek that Taylor rarely visited.

As father and daughter walked beside the creek around a bend, they came upon the opening to what seemed to be a long-deserted mine shaft. It was barely visible from the trail. The entrance was partially covered by overhanging vines and thick brush that had been torn away as a result of a recent violent storm.

Leaving his daughter just outside the entrance, Taylor fashioned a crude torch from some dry reeds and crawled into the shaft. Twenty yards deep into the mine, he came upon a thin vein of silver. The ore was so pure he was able to cut it from the rock with his pocketknife.

The next time Taylor went to St. Joe to purchase supplies and provisions, he paid with some of the silver. Startled, the storekeeper asked the farmer how he came by the precious metal. Taylor told the story of finding the old mine. Like Old Man Tabor decades before him, however, Taylor refused to provide details on the location. He did not want people coming onto his farm and disturbing his livestock, he explained. When word of the odd transaction spread through town, several old-timers familiar with the story of Old Man Tabor assumed Taylor had found the hermit's secret mine.

For several years, Taylor paid for food and items at the mercantile in St. Joe with silver dug from his mine. One day, while in town making his usual purchases, the clerk informed him they were no longer able to trade in silver. It had to be cash or coin. From that point on, Taylor used currency to pay for his goods. It was never known if he ever dug silver ore from the shaft again. Over the years, many attempted to get Taylor to reveal the location of the silver mine on his property, but he always refused. All that was known was that it was adjacent to Tomahawk Creek.

More time passed, and the Taylor property passed on to others. When interested parties inquired about the possibility of entering the area and searching for the old silver mine, the new owners stated they knew nothing about it and always refused admittance.

There is a great probability that Old Man Tabor's silver mine is still there, the vein of almost pure ore intact within. The current owners of the land through which Tomahawk Creek runs are most likely unaware of its existence. It is also quite possible that, with the passage of decades, the opening is covered over once again by overhanging vines and thick brush, lost as it once was and may be forevermore.

7.

The Lost Silver of Norristown Mountain

Norristown Mountain overlooks the Arkansas River near the town of Dardanelle. For generations, this promontory has served as an important landmark for travelers both by land and along this vitally important waterway. Today, the mountain overlooks dwellings, farms, and roads that stretch from its base across the lowlands toward the river.

Long before white settlers moved into this region, a tribe of Osage Indians lived here. To them, the mountain was scared. Historians have written that one of the largest Indian burial grounds in the nation begins at the foot of Norristown Mountain and stretches almost to the banks of the Arkansas River.

Attracted by the abundance of rich and fertile floodplain here, white settlers moved into the area in large numbers following the Civil War. With their encroachment, the Osage Indians were gradually pushed out of the region. Many of them resettled in Oklahoma, then known as Indian Territory. Initially, the Osage were determined to fight to keep their land from the whites, but they soon realized they were outnumbered and out-armed.

Confrontation would prove futile. Instead, the tribe sent a delegation to Washington, D.C. to negotiate a bargain to maintain possession of the mountain and the burial ground. A deal was made, and the Osage retained ownership for decades.

As the tribal elders passed away over the years, few of the remaining Osage maintained an interest in the Arkansas lands. Younger members of the tribe sought to leave the reservation and seek jobs in places such as Dallas, Oklahoma City, and St. Louis. Only a handful chose to return to Arkansas and live near Norristown Mountain.

Today, a few of the descendants of the original Osage still live in the area. Each year for many years, other descendants would journey from Oklahoma to the mountain, remain a few days or weeks for a celebration, then return home.

As time passed, governance of these Arkansas Osage lands was lax to nonexistent. The entire parcel was eventually purchased by a man named Peter Lovely. Lovely knew most of the Indians who lived in the area and got along well with them, becoming close friends with a number of the families. After the purchase, Lovely freely granted the Indians permission to continue to use the mountain for their gatherings and celebrations. The Osage were grateful.

From time to time, a small group of Osage would visit the Lovely homestead and present Mrs. Lovely with silver ornaments. The gifts consisted of beautiful handcrafted bracelets and necklaces. Mrs. Lovely wore the gifts with pride and often commented on the fine workmanship reflected in the pieces. Once, when she inquired as to the origin of the silver, the Indians pointed toward Norristown Mountain.

One afternoon, Mrs. Lovely was taking a walk along the bank of the Arkansas River when she spied a gathering of Indians just ahead. On nearing the group, she discovered they were involved in a burial ceremony. She stood back and watched. The Indian being interred was an old man who had visited her home on occasion and was well liked by her and her husband. He had been a prominent member of the tribe, and the ceremony was correspondingly elaborate, lasting for two hours.

Just before refilling the grave with dirt, the Indians, one by one, passed by the open excavation and dropped in offerings of handmade silver jewelry similar to that gifted to Mrs. Lovely. By the time they had finished, she estimated they had placed over a half-bushel of silver into the grave.

Following the burial, the Osage remained at the site and visited with one another. Mrs. Lovely approached, and she and an elderly woman soon became engaged in conversation. The woman told Mrs. Lovely that the old man had been a chief and was revered by the tribe. She said that many of the Indians in attendance had come from hundreds of miles away to honor him.

Mrs. Lovely commented that the members of the tribe must have dropped a fortune in silver into the grave. The old woman said that it was just a small amount of what came from the mine on the mountain. She gestured toward the top of Norristown Mountain as she spoke. She told Mrs. Lovely that if white men knew how much silver was in that mine that all of their horses would be shod with silver.

For all of her virtues, Mrs. Lovely could not keep this information regarding the silver mine to herself. She repeated to others what the old woman had said, and soon the story of the rich silver mine atop Norristown Mountain was on the lips of most people living in that portion of the Arkansas River Valley. As normally happens when stories such as this become common knowledge, prospectors and fortune hunters began making their way to the mountaintop.

Although a great deal of excavation took place, no one ever found anything of value. Before long, men were claiming that the story of the silver atop Norristown Mountain was a hoax, a diversionary tactic employed by the Indians to misdirect any white men who sought the mine. Finding nothing, the hopeful miners would depart the area, never to return.

Years later, Mrs. Lovely mentioned this strategy to one of the Osage that had been friendly to her and her husband and asked it was true. The Indian only laughed and said the white men would never find the silver mine because it was elaborately concealed, its location known only to select members of the tribe. And yes, it was on the top of Norristown Mountain.

In 1926, a man arrived in Russellville. He had the look of a gypsy and drove a rickety old wagon pulled by two scrawny mules. He set up a temporary camp on the south bank of the Arkansas River. During a conversation with one of the locals, the stranger identified himself as a Spaniard and said he was interested in doing some prospecting. Though he never showed it to anyone, it was said that the newcomer possessed a very old map that indicated the location of a buried treasure.

Over the next few days, the stranger was seen walking around the old Osage burial ground, stopping now and then to consult his map. After a full week of searching, he hired two men from town to do some digging for him. One night around midnight, the stranger guided the two diggers out to the burial ground. One of his mules was laden with shovels and a packsaddle with stout leather packs.

On arriving at a pre-selected spot, the stranger lit a lantern, studied the map, checked nearby landmarks, and ordered the men to dig. During the next two hours, the group excavated several holes in the immediate area until at last they unearthed a cache of silver artifacts, mostly ornaments and jewelry. The workers later revealed that the stranger removed all of the silver and placed it in the leather packs. He then ordered the diggers to refill all of the holes and to never reveal to anyone what they had found. The stranger told them that he would return in two days and present each of the diggers an extra stipend for their effort.

Two weeks passed, and the stranger never returned. The two diggers believed they had been swindled and grew upset. It was at that point that they told others what transpired that night. The Spaniard was never seen again in the area.

An old man who lived in the shadow of Norristown Mountain during the 1980s had earned a reputation as a competent and reliable dowser. He had helped a number of area farmers with the placement of wells on their properties. The dowser claimed he was also able to locate precious metals such as silver and gold. As a dowser, he said, he took no money for his work. Instead, he lived on welfare and food stamps.

The old man told friends that one day, as a result of his dowsing, he had found several small chunks of silver at the top of Norristown Mountain. He offered the opinion that they most likely came from the lost Indian mine alleged to be located there. He said the silver was scattered about the top of the mountain.

The dowser had a theory about the Osage silver mine. He said a mine is often easy to spot because there is usually a pile of tailings just outside the opening. He suggested that as the Indians dug silver out of the mine and enlarged the shaft, they carried the tailings out in buckets and distributed them across the mountaintop to remove any evidence of their activity. He believed the pieces of silver he located were undetected nuggets that had been dumped from the buckets.

Some who have heard the old man's claims have asked to see the silver he took from the mountain. He refused, causing some to doubt his story. A few years after he began dowsing for silver on the mountaintop, however, the old man somehow came up with enough money to purchase a forty-acre farm a few miles downriver as well as a brand new pickup truck each year for several years in a row. He paid for all of his purchases with cash. Those who knew the dowser well suggested he enjoyed considerable success searching for and recovering silver nuggets atop the mountain.

The Osage who live in the area today claim that the silver can only be removed from the mine by someone who intends to use it for the good of the tribe. Those who wish to profit from the ore, they say, will never find it. The Osage also claim that at some time in the future there may be a need for the silver. Until then, it is intended that it rest quietly at its secret location on Norristown Mountain overlooking the Arkansas River.

8.

Turtle Rock Treasure

During the late 1800s and early 1900s, people living in and around Pope County heard numerous tales, legends, and lore regarding lost Spanish treasure alleged to have been buried in the area. One of the stories, as it was handed down in families and communities, related that the Iberians mined, processed, and buried gold and silver in the region of Piney Creek between Pilot Rock Mountain and Ford Mountain. One of the most fascinating of these tales involves what the locals referred to as the "turtle rock treasure."

Around 1910, as the late Piney Page told it, an old man named Mose Freeman set out early one morning to gather his corn crop. For years, Freeman planted corn on the broad floodplain associated with Piney Creek where it makes a wide horseshoe-shaped bend between the two mountains. Moments after he arrived that day, he spotted two men camped in the woods near the far end of his field. When he had harvested a significant portion of his crop, Freeman took a break and walked over to the camp to visit with the two men. He was interested in learning if they brought any news from beyond the valley. Visitors were rare in the Piney Creek region, and Mose always enjoyed the company of passers-by.

As Freeman approached the two men, he noted that they seemed nervous and evasive. One of them was a short and mean-looking half-Indian with a scar that ran down the entire length of his face. The other man was tall and gangly and seemed subordinate to the shorter man.

When it was clear that Freeman had spotted the two men, they stepped forward and voiced a rather reserved greeting. After a few minutes of conversation, the shorter man told the farmer he wanted to ask him a few questions about the area. Freeman told him he'd lived in the valley longer than anyone and knew pretty much everything there was to know about it.

The short man asked Freeman if he knew of any old carvings of turtles or snakes on exposed rocks in the area. Freeman thought for a moment, scratched the stubble on his chin, and finally said he had never seen any such thing. The three men visited for another several minutes, and then Freeman stated he needed to get back to work. He bade his visitors a good day and returned to gathering his corn.

Four days later, as Freeman was harvesting some eggs from his henhouse, he saw the two strangers again. This time they were riding in a wagon piled high with camping gear and pulled by two horses that appeared to be half-starved. They were on their way out of the valley. Both men carried rifles, and as they rode along they cast fearful glances around them as if they were protecting something in the wagon. After leaving the valley, the two men were never seen again.

The following morning, Freeman and one of his sons walked down to the cornfield. After repairing a sagging fence, they entered the woods where the two men had camped. Freeman said he wanted to have a look. The deserted camp was a poor one, and

Freeman saw nothing of significance. A short distance away, however, the son spotted several holes that had been dug into the ground around a large beech tree.

As the two men peered at the holes and wondered why on earth they had been dug, Freeman glanced up at the trunk of the tree and saw the weathered figure of a snake that had been carved deep into the wood. The head of the snake was pointed downward.

One hundred feet north of the beech tree, Freeman came across a large rock that looked as if it had recently been dug out of the ground, turned over, then set back down atop its original location. With the help of his son and a stout limb they used as a lever, Freeman turned the rock over. On the newly exposed side was a large carved image of a turtle.

The rock had been laid over a newly excavated hole about two feet deep. In one corner of the excavation, they saw a smaller hole from which it appeared something about the size of a cooking pot had been removed. Over the years, Freeman had heard tales of Spanish treasure buried in the area, but he never believed them. The farmer was now beginning to think there was more to the stories than he realized. It appeared to him that the two strangers had found what they were searching for.

Over the years, Mose Freeman told the story of the two strangers and the odd carvings on tree and rock to several people. He learned that the early Spanish explorers often used the figures of snakes and turtles to indicate nearby locations of hidden wealth, usually in the form of gold or silver. The head of the snake or turtle always pointed to the location of the treasure. Freeman learned from some of his neighbors that they remembered seeing other such images carved on rocks in the area, but this had occurred years earlier and none could remember exactly where they were located.

In 1976, a geology professor associated with a small Missouri college was conducting a field studies class in the southern Ozarks. He and his students spent several days camping in and exploring around Piney Creek and Moccasin Creek Valley in Pope County. They were studying the unique stratigraphy of Ozark limestone and collecting fossil specimens. The professor instructed the students to keep journals of their observations. He also required them to maintain photographic records of their activities. After eight days of research and study, the class returned to Missouri.

Several weeks later, while the professor was in his office examining the journals, notes, and photographic records of his pupils, one particular image captured his attention. Among the materials submitted by a young female student was a photograph of a thick limestone slab the size of a large sofa cushion. On the top of it, the dim outline of a turtle could be seen. The only visible landmark in the photograph was a thick oak tree located not far from the rock.

The geology professor had heard many stories of buried treasure in the Arkansas Ozarks; he was also familiar with certain signs and symbols used by the Spanish to indicate such sites. As a result, he grew excited about the photograph. When he contacted the student, however, he learned she had not noted the precise location of the rock she had photographed. When the professor unrolled a topographic map of the area and attempted to get her to recall the approximate area where she saw the rock, she was unable to provide any pertinent information.

At the first opportunity, the professor returned to Moccasin Creek Valley in Pope County to search for the rock. He retraced many of the trails and paths he and his students followed previously, but he was never able to find it. During subsequent years, he conducted other classes in the area, always reminding his students to keep an eye out for a limestone slab marked with the image of a turtle. To date, no one has found it. The professor, now retired, still searches.

9.

Confederate Soldier's Gold

During the Civil War, Corporal Henry Fletcher served in a company of Confederate troops. The unit was riding to join another contingent of cavalry near the tiny community of Sugar Grove in western Arkansas. The day was pleasant, and the troopers were working their way leisurely through Brushy Creek Valley in the Ouachita Mountains.

Each side of the valley was bordered by the low-rolling and gentle hills of the sandstone and shale of this mountain range. Here and there, the soldiers spotted a few isolated farmhouses and cattle grazing in the meadows and creek bottoms. Brushy Creek was a shallow, slow-flowing stream of clear, spring-fed water that wound for miles through the long narrow valley, providing water for area cattle herds.

At one point during the passage through Brushy Creek Valley, Corporal Fletcher became ill. He told his commanding officer that he needed to lie down for a while. The officer granted permission, telling Fletcher to catch up with the company when he recovered. The corporal dropped back and watched his fellow troopers ride away, disappearing around a bend in the distance. Fletcher guided his mount toward the shade of a nearby sandstone bluff from which flowed a tiny spring.

After dismounting, Fletcher unsaddled his horse and staked it out to graze on some lush grasses that grew along the narrow watercourse that ran from the spring to Brushy Creek. He then walked over to the spring to slake his thirst. As he brought water to his mouth with his cupped palm, he was distracted by a glint of color in a vein of quartz that ran through an outcrop of a different kind of rock extruding through the sandstone.

After slaking his thirst, Fletcher walked over to the rock and found it to be part of a granite outcrop that had been exposed as a result of eons of erosion having removed the softer, less resistant sandstone that overlaid it. The quartz was brittle, and the golden color that weaved through it was strange to him. His curiosity aroused, Fletcher knocked some of it loose with the butt of his pistol and placed it in his knapsack. He napped in the shade for an hour, drank more water, and then, feeling somewhat better, saddled his mount and rode away to rejoin his companions.

Several weeks passed, and Fletcher's company was sent to Fort Smith. When he was allowed some time off, Fletcher took the rock samples from his knapsack and carried them to an assayer. The trooper was told that the quartz contained a high grade of gold ore.

Fletcher was excited at the prospect of having discovered a deposit of gold in the Ouachita Mountains. He realized he could be a wealthy man. Because of his military commitment, however, he was unable to return to Brushy Creek Valley and to the low bluff where he had found the spring. His excitement was further quelled when he realized he still had a year and a half until his enlistment was up.

Time passed, and within days after being discharged from the army, Fletcher traveled to Fort Smith. There, he purchased some mining tools, camping equipment, and two mules. A few days later he returned to Brushy Creek Valley. His intention was to travel directly to the low bluff with the spring and begin excavating the gold-laden quartz.

On arriving at the valley, Fletcher became disoriented. It was not as he remembered it, and he had difficulty recognizing landmarks. A recent flood had also changed the appearance of the valley floor, somewhat altering the course of Brushy Creek at several locations. Furthermore, extensive timber cutting had laid bare large sections of the hillsides and slopes.

Confused and disoriented, Fletcher nevertheless undertook his search for the bluff that contained the gold-bearing quartz. For three weeks, he rode back and forth across the valley, inspecting every likely outcrop he encountered. He eventually exhausted his already meager resources and was forced to return to Fort Smith. There, he obtained a grubstake and set forth once again in search of the gold. His second trip was likewise a failure. For yet a third time he obtained some minimal financing and rode back to Brushy Creek Valley to find his fortune, but it continued to elude him.

Months passed without success, but Fletcher doggedly pursued his search, stopping only to return to Fort Smith to resupply. By this time, the story of his search for the elusive vein of gold near the bluff was widely known throughout western Arkansas. As a result, Fletcher would sometimes encounter other prospectors and gold seekers during his own explorations.

The months turned into years. Continually living in the open and existing on poor rations began to take its toll on Fletcher. He was stricken with a bout of pneumonia. Believing it would pass, he continued to search for the gold but only became weaker. One day, a farmer found Fletcher lying on the ground unconscious. He had passed out near Brushy Creek during a driving rainstorm and had lain exposed for several hours, aggravating his already debilitating condition. He was transported to the hospital at Fort Smith. There, he remained for several weeks before being deemed fit enough for release. Fletcher moved into a room in town, determined to regain his health and continue his search. It was not to happen. A few months after he was discharged from the hospital, Henry Fletcher died from complications related to pneumonia.

Skeptics have insisted that gold cannot be found in the sandstone-dominated Ouachita Mountains, that such rock is not conducive to the formation of this precious metal. As a result, they claim, the story of Henry Fletcher's gold is a hoax.

The skeptics are wrong. It has been proven time and again that beneath the sandstone layers of the Ouachitas, arms of intrusive igneous rock made their way into the fractures and fissures of the softer, more brittle sedimentary rock ages ago—seams of granite that, under the right conditions, yielded gold. Over time, the softer sandstone eroded, exposing the granite and its pockets of precious ore.

In fact, gold has been found in the Ouachitas on a number of occasions over the decades. Twelve years after the death of Henry Fletcher, newspapers carried the story that gold had been discovered at Redman's Mill in Brushy Creek Valley and gave rise to a burgeoning town—Golden City—that flourished for a short time and then expired. The subsequent mining operations that were undertaken, however, were on Redman's farm property and nowhere near a sandstone bluff. Fletcher's discovery had still not been found. During the 1880s, a commercial gold mining operation was established in the eastern Ouachita Mountains, but the vein was exhausted after only a few months.

In 1985, a Brushy Creek Valley farmer claimed to know where Fletcher's lost bluff was located. He said the vein was found in an outcrop of granite near his property and not far from a small dripping spring. He further claimed that he has dug gold from the vein himself but insists that there is not enough to warrant a full-fledged mining operation. He is also fearful that if such a mine were established in the valley, it would disrupt his farming operations as well as those of his neighbors. He recalled stories of the boom-and-bust disturbance of the Redman farm discovery during the 1880s and does not wish to see such a thing repeated.

In spite of the farmer's wishes, there has been a renewed interest in the possibility of finding gold in Brushy Creek Valley among some geologists who want to sink exploratory shafts. They are confident there is enough gold in the valley to support commercial mining activity.

This remains to be seen. To date, the search is ongoing with no discoveries of gold yet reported. So far, the quest adds to the growing legend of gold, lost and found, in the peaceful setting of Brushy Creek Valley.

10.

The Crystal Hill Gold Mine

The historical record reveals that the Spanish explorer Hernando de Soto, while surveying parts of the American South, led his command along a route that followed the Arkansas River to a location known today as Little Rock. After establishing a camp here, he sent men into the Ozark and Ouachita Mountains to prospect for precious metals, primarily gold and silver. Though evidence of Spanish mining has been found throughout these two mountain ranges, none had ever been located near their Little Rock encampment.

Then in 1909, a man named Trammell was prospecting a location known as Crystal Hill, described at the time as "a short boat ride upriver from downtown Little Rock." Trammell was intrigued by a variety of geological aspects of some rock outcrops he found there and spent several weeks examining their potential. One day he encountered a quartz vein running through some exposed rock. On close examination, he detected gold in the quartz. Excited, Trammell announced his discovery, and in a short time this low mountain was swarming with dozens of prospectors.

Intrigued by the potential for a profitable gold mining operation, investors and entrepreneurs immediately entered the scene. Within weeks, several boatloads of mining equipment were transported up the Arkansas River from New Orleans, unloaded at the river port of Little Rock, and carried by wagon to Crystal Hill. Several mining camps were established on the low mountain as well as along the foothills.

One miner known as Captain Hillaire sank several exploratory shafts into the mountain in search of gold. Traces of the ore were found with each attempt but none in enough quantity to justify a fully developed mining operation. Hillaire subsequently hired Trammell to show him the original site where he had found the gold-laden quartz. Here, more exploratory shafts were sunk and gold was found. Soon, a small smelter was constructed next to this series of shafts.

Mining progressed for several months until the vein of gold thinned out and then disappeared altogether. With the venture no longer profitable, Hillaire broke down his equipment and moved out of the area.

After that time, weekend prospectors from Little Rock traveled the short distance to Crystal Hill and hunted for gold. On a good afternoon, one could sometimes find a few small nuggets to make the labor worthwhile. This activity went on for years, and then the Crystal Hill region was subjected to residential development. During the construction of homes and roads in the area, workers would occasionally report the discovery of gold nuggets. In 1998, a Crystal Hill resident found a large chunk of gold while working in her flower garden.

Not far from the Crystal Hill area are the remains of the Kellogg lead mines. The mining company excavated and processed lead ore at this site before shipping it to a market that had been established in Europe. Under mysterious circumstances no one quite understands today, the company closed down the mines and abandoned the area.

In addition to lead, it was discovered, a significant amount of silver was also mined at this location. An old report contains details of the discovery of a lump of silver that weighed 108 pounds. For several years following the closing of the Kellogg mines, freelance prospectors arrived at the area and dug impressive amounts of silver from the abandoned shafts.

Today, those who are familiar with the stories of the Crystal Hill and Kellogg mines travel to the area and, with some patient searching, occasionally find a nugget or two.

11.

The Lost Bear Creek Silver Mine

The town of Huntsville is located in northwestern Arkansas deep in the Ozark Mountains. Densely wooded hills, shaded hollows, and shallow winding creeks supplied by ample spring water characterize the region. Throughout history, this area has been a favorite hiding place for outlaws, bootleggers, and moonshiners. These days, people earn a living from logging, farming, and a bit of tourist traffic.

Old-time Huntsville residents relate tales of lost mines or buried treasures that can allegedly be found here, but most are vague about details. And most current residents have little knowledge of what turned out to be a relatively famous lost mine that made newspaper headlines throughout the state in 1936.

Many people living in the area of Huntsville learned about the silver mine when two local counterfeiters were arrested. During the subsequent trial, both men admitted they had manufactured phony silver dollars from ore they dug from their "secret" mine. For months, they passed the counterfeit dollars at stores and taverns throughout the area. The fake coins were detected when a sharp-eyed banker noticed that one that came into his possession was slightly thicker than those produced by the United States mint.

Part of the story told by the counterfeiters in court related the existence of what was by their account a rich silver mine. Not surprisingly, it generated one of the most intensive searches ever to occur in the state of Arkansas, a search that continues to this day.

When questioned, the two men admitted that they had learned about the existence of the silver mine many years earlier from an old man named Elliot. Elliot, in turn, told them that mining was first undertaken by Spaniards who had arrived in the region centuries earlier. By the time the trial of the two counterfeiters got underway, Elliot had been deceased for several years. Some of the older residents of Huntsville recalled that Elliot himself had manufactured and passed counterfeit dollars in the region for several years following the Civil War.

The two counterfeiters stated that Elliot took them to the mine and showed them how to extract the ore. In addition, he showed them how to make wooden molds employed to fashion the fake coins.

In court, the two defendants said the silver they dug out of the mine was nearly pure and could easily be hammered out into thin sheets. They also claimed that the mine was within a half-day walk from the Madison County courthouse where they were standing trial. The two men further stated that they carried the silver ore in sacks to a location in Bear Creek Hollow, ten miles northeast of Huntsville and not far from the small community of Forum. Bear Creek Hollow was a remote location seldom visited by anyone. In times past, a lot of whiskey had been illegally distilled there, utilizing the clear waters of the creek. Moonshiners and their customers would often meet in Bear Creek Hollow to arrange purchases. According to some nearby residents, a few moonshiners were still active during the 1930s, and they may have worked side-by-side with the counterfeiters.

Despite aggressive questioning by law enforcement authorities, the accused men refused to reveal the location of the silver mine. They claimed it was well hidden and that unless one knew exactly where to look it would be almost impossible to locate.

Some who have researched the tale of the old silver mine in depth are convinced that it was not located a half-day walk from Huntsville at all, but actually in Bear Creek Hollow. They claim that the two men made up the story of the location near Huntsville to divert and confuse anyone who might want to go search for it. Researchers also point to an obscure reference in an old historical society journal that mentions the mining of silver in Bear Creek Hollow in 1886.

According to their testimony, the counterfeiters, on accumulating a significant amount of the ore, melted it down and rolled it out into sheets about the thickness of a coin. They set a mold atop the sheet of the soft silver and hammered it with a mallet, thus forming a coin and imposing an image on one side. They turned the coin over and hammered another image on the opposite side. They grooved the edges of the coins by hand.

Those who inspected the wooden molds fashioned by the two men testified that they were well made and that the images stamped onto the coins were difficult to distinguish from real ones issued by the federal government. Interestingly, an analysis of the counterfeit coins revealed that they contained a higher quantity of silver than those minted by the United States, and as a result were actually worth more. Today, these rare coins would be regarded as prized collector items.

One of the defendants claimed there was enough silver in the mine to pave every road in the state of Arkansas.

Both men were convicted of counterfeiting and sentenced to several years of hard labor at Cummins Prison Farm, southeast of Little Rock. During their incarceration, the sheriff of Madison County drove to the Cummins Unit on several occasions to visit with the two convicts. On each occasion, he tried to persuade the prisoners to reveal the location of the silver mine in exchange for a lighter sentence. The prisoners were convinced, however, that the sheriff wanted the knowledge of the location for himself and that he had no authority to reduce their prison terms. The men remained silent on the subject during their entire sentence.

When it came time for the two men to be released, several Huntsville residents anticipated their return, hoping they would have an opportunity to secretly follow them to the silver mine. On the day of their discharge, however, they left for California. According to relatives, the two never set foot in Arkansas again.

Today, people still search for what has come to be called the Lost Huntsville Silver Mine. Most of the searches have focused on Bear Creek Hollow, but to date the mine remains lost.

12.

The Lost Aztec Mine

Franklin County is located in northwestern Arkansas near the southern limit of the Ozark Mountains, where the foothills grade toward the Arkansas River. This country has been the setting for several fascinating tales of Indians, outlaws, and ghosts. The most unusual story, however, is one that purports the existence of gold mines that were once operated in that area by the Aztec Indians.

This notion is bizarre for a number of reasons, not the least of which is the fact that the homeland of the Aztecs is well over one thousand miles to the south in Mexico. It would seem on the surface that it is quite unlikely that members of a Meso-American Indian tribe would travel such a distance to mine gold, but the legends persist.

Such tales are not without skeptics, and those who would dismiss such stories as nonsense point to the fact that there has never been any physical evidence of the presence of Aztecs in the Ozarks. At least, not according to the academic archeologists.

For years, however, mysterious petroglyphs have been found in several remote areas of the Ozarks. The origins of these inscriptions clearly predate the settlement of the region by the Osage and

Quapaw. In spite of what the archeologists say, a few observers have pointed out that the glyphs bear a striking resemblance to Aztec symbols found deep in Mexico.

There exists, in fact, a surprising amount of evidence for Aztec presence in the United States. A number of professional archeologists are convinced that this tribe, in fact, originated in the southwestern U.S. and then migrated into Mexico where it established a new and successful homeland. Having had experience mining gold and silver as well as precious stones in the American Southwest—all used for fashioning ornaments and idols—and not having access to such in equal abundance in their newer residence, the Aztecs often journeyed back to locations in present-day Arizona and New Mexico where they conducted mining activities. This being the case, it is not out of the realm of possibility that the tribe might have wandered into what is now Arkansas.

As recently as 1986, an odd discovery was made atop Wolverton Mountain, a flat-topped, narrow sandstone ridge located in northern Conway County. Several farmers living on the mountain were battling a fire and had plowed a firebreak between the forest and a grass field. As the plow cut through a shallow layer of soil, it kicked up a small carved stone figure of a man. The style of the carving was primitive and decidedly Meso-American. It bore a remarkable similarity to carvings unearthed during excavations of Aztec sites in Mexico. Several experts who have seen the stone figure have tentatively identified it as being Indian, most likely Aztec.

The skeptics were quick to respond by saying that the carving could have been dropped by area Indians following trade with Aztecs somewhere in Mexico. While the carving may not entirely prove Aztec visitation in the Ozarks, it does open the door to speculation that such an event could have occurred.

Skeptics of an earlier era had no influence on a man who lived in Franklin County. His name was O.P. Van Brunt (sometimes seen spelled as VanBrunt), and he claimed he had reason to believe that the Aztecs visited this region long ago in search of precious metals. Van Brunt, a resident of the small town of Mulberry, located where the Mulberry River meets the Arkansas River, has searched for lost gold mines in the Ozarks for decades. Based on his efforts, he became convinced that a fortune in gold was hidden in a tunnel excavated into a hill in the northeastern part of the county not far from the Mulberry River.

Van Brunt's father had searched for many years for this tunnel, beginning in 1918. Like others in the area, he referred to it as a lost Spanish mine and associated it with the Spanish explorers who visited the region during the sixteenth century.

A prevailing Arkansas legend, however, states that when the Spanish arrived in this area they encountered Aztec Indians mining gold here. Some have said that the Spaniards drove the Aztecs away. Other claim the Indians were all slain by the Spaniards. In either case, so the legend goes, the Spaniards took over the mines that had been worked by the Aztecs and dug gold from them for years.

It was further said that the Spanish remained there until the war with France broke out in Europe. There was a growing fear the conflict would extend to the Americas. Since there were a number of French settlements in Arkansas at the time, the Spaniards decided to abandon the area before their mines and the gold could be seized. Before leaving, however, they covered the entrances to the mines so they would not be easily detected by anyone who chanced by.

Despite the departure of the Spaniards, the story of the lost mines lived on in the Ozarks, passed down over the generations by the resident Indians. When white settlers moved into the region during the middle to latter part of the nineteenth century, they heard these tales of lost gold. Many dismissed them as fanciful Indian yarns, but others set forth into the Ozarks in search of them.

In 1915, a Franklin County physician named L.G. Hill grew enthralled by the stories of lost gold in the Ozarks since many of them centered on the area close to his home near the Mulberry River. In particular, he was fascinated with one they referred to as the Lost Aztec Mine.

In his later years, Dr. Hill related a story about an encounter he had with an old man, a Spaniard named Antonio, who was traveling through the Ozarks. The stranger rode up to Dr. Hill's residence on a worn-out horse, knocked on the door, and asked if he could purchase a meal. The old man was clearly tired and hungry, and Hill invited him for dinner. Following the meal, Hill invited the Spaniard into his study to visit. It was not often that company arrived at the Hill residence unless it was related to some form of medical treatment or emergency. Hill was anxious to learn of the Spaniard's travels and any news he might have picked up along the way.

The old man asked Hill about several landmarks in the area he said he was searching for. The physician provided directions and asked his visitor the reason for his interest. Hill was stunned when the old man said he was searching for an old Spanish gold mine. He said he had learned of the existence of the gold from relatives in Spain. Before he had left for the United States, they provided him with information of the symbols and writings, carved into the Ozark rock, that would guide him to the treasure.

The Spaniard asked Dr. Hill for a paper and pencil and was brought the items forthwith. On the paper, the old man sketched several of the symbols as he remembered them. To Hill's astonishment, he recognized them as markings on some limestone cliffs a few miles upstream of his residence. Hill made no mention of this fact to the Spaniard.

Dr. Hill invited the old man to spend the night. With gratitude, he accepted. The following morning after a hearty breakfast, the Spaniard rode away. He was never seen again by the physician.

Hill's fascination with the lost treasure and the mines never waned. In 1918, he organized the Lonquil Mining Company. Along with several associates, he searched the Ozark Mountains throughout Franklin County for the legendary gold mine for years, but he had no success.

O.P. Van Brunt related the fact that his father was one of the investors in the Lonquil Mining Company. Van Brunt recalled a time when he was six years old and went on a trip with his father by horse-drawn wagon. They drove out to a remote portion of the Ozarks in Franklin County and remained for two weeks. Van Brunt recalled they camped near a hill, and it was to this landform that his father devoted most of his attention. The father dug at several different locations along the side of the hill searching, he told his son, for the opening to a tunnel that, according to legend, held an enormous cache of gold.

At the time, the young Van Brunt was too unsophisticated to appreciate the importance of the activity and contented himself with exploring around the camp. He did recall, however, that at one point his father found a large piece of rock that was "speckled" with gold. There was enough gold in the rock, he said, for his father to make two wedding bands.

When Van Brunt grew to be a man, he never forgot about his father's quest to find the lost tunnel and the treasure cache. Working at various jobs to earn a living limited his opportunities to renew the search, but his interest never waned.

Van Brunt was able to resume his search for the treasure in 1973. He concentrated on McIlroy Mountain in the northeastern part of Franklin County. He learned from others that several caves could be found in this mountain, and some area residents had reported the existence of ancient man-made tunnels there, evidence of mining.

A man named Jesse Jones owned most of McIlroy Mountain. He and Van Brunt worked out an arrangement such that the latter leased the right to conduct excavations. Jones, like Van Brunt, was convinced that gold lay somewhere in the mountain, gold that was once mined by the Aztecs.

Jones was certain that he had once found the entrance to what he referred to as the "Doc Hill Mine." He claimed it was on the western side of the mountain not far from the Mulberry River. The drift, he said, measured six feet by six feet and penetrated the mountain to a depth of almost 150 feet. At places inside the drift, Jones continued, could be found very old timbers that were used for shoring. Not far from the opening to the drift, Jones saw a number of very old signs and symbols scratched into the rock. Jones was certain the symbols had been inscribed by the Aztecs.

Jones claimed he found what he described as a "small wheel" made from gold not far from the entrance to this tunnel. He sent the object to someone who promised to have it identified and evaluated, but he never heard from the man again.

Jones explained that the rocks associated with McIlroy Mountain are different from others in the area in that they possess a "rusty" tinge. When the sun is at a certain angle, he said, the rock takes on a color similar to that of blood.

Regarding the blood-red color of the rock, Jones related an aspect of the lost treasure legend many have not heard before. He said that the version of the tale he heard had the mountain stained forever by the blood of the slain Aztecs. He further stated that the mountain is cursed, and it is not likely that it will relinquish the gold found deep within.

Why then, he was asked, did he allow Van Brunt to search for the gold? Jones explained there was always a possibility someone might beat the curse, and that his friend might be the one. Jones neglected to mention that his arrangement with Van Brunt entitled him to a large percentage of any discovery.

Another question put to Jones had to do with his knowledge of the location of the drift. If he knew where it was, why did he not retrieve the gold himself? He answered that the drift had been covered up by a landslide and that it would require expensive heavy equipment to reopen it.

Until such time as the mysterious drift is breached, the alleged immense treasure of the Aztecs still lies within.

13.

McCord's Lost White River Gold Mine

Somewhere in Baxter County, located in the north-central part of the state, is a small but productive gold mine whose location seems to have been known to only one man. With his death went knowledge of the location of the mine, but people continue to search for it to this day. The most accessible route to this mine is by way of the White River.

Sometime during the 1940s, a man named Gordon Lambrecht became friends with another he knew only as McCord. Lambrecht and McCord both liked to fish and began spending long days together on the lakes and rivers of the area in and around Baxter County. This went on for more than a year.

One afternoon, McCord asked Lambrecht if he would like to accompany him to a secret location where he dug gold from a small mine. Lambrecht was intrigued at this notion and agreed.

One morning a week later, McCord, driving an old pickup truck, arrived at Lambrecht's house and told him he was prepared to take him to his gold mine to dig some of the ore. Lambrecht took a few minutes to lace up his boots and find his coat and then joined

McCord in the truck. McCord drove to the town of Cotter, located near the White River. At a commercial boat dock, they rented a craft from a man McCord knew. McCord transferred some supplies and tools from the truck into the boat, started the motor, and steered upstream.

After thirty minutes of travel, McCord turned the boat into the mouth of a narrow, shallow stream that entered the river from the east. Taking care to avoid floating branches, McCord followed the stream for five hundred feet until it became too shallow to proceed. After banking the craft and tying its rope to a tree, the two men gathered up the tools. McCord led Lambrecht along a seldom-used trail that wound its way to the top of a low hill for six hundred feet. On either side of the trail, dense brush prevailed. McCord proudly told Lambrecht that he had hacked out the path himself.

Once at the top of the hill, McCord pointed to a shallow hole. Here, according to Lambrecht, there was evidence of recent excavation. For several minutes, McCord described the geologic processes that gave rise to the kind of rock extruding through the limestone cap. Lambrecht was impressed with McCord's knowledge of geology. Gesturing toward the excavation, McCord showed Lambrecht a vein of quartz running across the length of the exposed rock. Leading Lambrecht over to it, McCord pointed out the tiny particles of gold that could be seen within the quartz.

Following McCord's directions, Lambrecht began digging away at the vein and the adjacent rock. Now and then, McCord would call a halt to the digging. He would drop to his knees and run his hands through the shattered pieces of quartz, occasionally retrieving a small nugget of gold that he would place in his shirt pocket. For three hours, the men worked at the small mine before McCord called a halt and said it was time to return to the creek.

Once back at the little stream, McCord withdrew two metal pans from his pack and showed Lambrecht how to pan for gold from the sands and gravel of the bottom. For the next two hours, the two men harvested a number of tiny gold nuggets.

The two friends returned to the boat dock at sundown. McCord took Lambrecht home and said he would see him the following morning. True to his word, McCord showed up around nine A.M. and presented Lambrecht twenty dollars for his assistance at recovering gold the previous day.

Lambrecht was fascinated with the idea that a gold mine could be found not far from where he lived. Though he wanted to travel to the mine and dig out some of the gold, he felt that McCord had ownership. McCord never took Lambrecht back to the mine.

Time passed, and one day Lambrecht, while reading the obituaries in the morning paper, learned that McCord had died. Several weeks following this, Lambrecht decided he would try to relocate his late friend's gold mine. Like the time he went with McCord, Lambrecht drove to the same dock, rented a boat, and steered it upriver in search of the narrow stream that entered from the east. Lambrecht recalled that during that earlier trip they traveled for approximately thirty minutes before reaching the stream.

Lambrecht passed several small tributaries on his way upriver. After thirty minutes, he turned into the next one he came to. He went upstream only a short distance before realizing it was not the right one. He explored the next with no success—and the next, and the next. Clearly, none of the streams he entered was the one he and McCord had traveled. Lambrecht turned and went back downstream, exploring other streams he had passed on the way up. No luck. Frustrated and discouraged, Lambrecht returned to the boat dock.

Lambrecht searched for the stream on at least six other occasions but was no more successful than he was on his first trip. It continued to elude him. Finally, he decided he was not meant to find it. Lambrecht told the story of his search for the gold mine to others. Other men attempted to find it over the next several years, but all reported failure.

Somewhere atop a low hill overlooking a narrow, shallow stream, a tributary to the White River, is a small but productive gold mine—one that has, according to Lambrecht, the potential to make someone rich. The mine has eluded discovery for more than seventy years.

14.

Lost Gold Mine in Crawford County

During the year 1904, a group of a dozen Ozark Mountain residents was cutting trees in Crawford County in northwest Arkansas. They worked in the area of White Rock Mountain. As was their practice, they drove wagons out to a selected site, set up a camp near the banks of Hurricane Creek, and worked for several weeks cutting and harvesting timber. The spring-fed Hurricane Creek provided clear cool water for drinking and washing.

One evening, as the timber cutters were seated around the campfire resting from their day of labor and eating their supper, a large party of Mexicans arrived in wagons, carts, on horseback, and on foot. There were about thirty of them, including two elderly men and several women and children. One of the Mexicans approached the timber cutters and politely requested permission to set up camp along Hurricane Creek not far from them so that they might utilize the waters of the stream as well. The timber cutters assented and even helped the newcomers unload their wagons.

As the Mexicans went about the business of establishing their camp, they unloaded a number of mining tools from the wagons.

When they had set up their tents and other shelters—seemingly in preparation for an extended stay—a few of the Mexicans entered into conversation with the several of the timber cutters. In broken English, one of the newcomers explained that they had traveled for many weeks from a location deep in Mexico. Several months earlier, he said, they had come into possession of an ancient map showing the location of a gold mine not far from that very campsite. The map had been drawn by a Spaniard named Alvarez who was a member of an earlier expedition that had come to this location. In addition to the map, the men had also obtained a sheaf of directions from Alvarez.

According to the information possessed by the Mexicans, the mine was very rich. Their ancestors, who had been enslaved by the Spaniards and brought to the area to work in the mine, had excavated a shaft and extracted the gold. The Mexicans intended to locate the old shaft and extract as much ore as possible before returning home.

The timber cutters listened to the story with interest but had doubts about the existence of a gold mine in the area. They had all lived nearby for years and had never heard of such a thing. They had traveled throughout the hills and valleys of the region and had never seen anything resembling a mine. They wished the Mexicans luck in their search and returned to their own camp.

During the next few days, several of the younger Mexicans, maps and directions in hand, set out on foot into the surrounding mountains in search of the mine. One evening several days after arriving, one of them announced he had found it. The following day, the Mexicans broke their camp and moved it from Hurricane Creek to a location in a steep-walled canyon about a mile away.

For the next few days, the timber cutters saw little of the Mexicans save for the occasions when some of the women drove a wagon to the creek to fill water barrels. In the distance, however, they heard dynamite blasts several times each day. One afternoon when the women were filling water barrels, one of the timber cutters approached and inquired about the progress with the mine. One of the women explained that all of the men were busy working in the mine and excavating the gold.

Time passed, and one evening as the timber cutters were eating dinner, the leader mentioned he had not heard any dynamite blasts that day. For another two days they heard nothing at all from the remote canyon, nor did the women come to the creek any longer. The following afternoon, a pair of timber cutters decided to venture into the canyon to check on the Mexicans. On arriving, they encountered only an abandoned campsite. The newcomers had departed. The timber cutters located the mine shaft nearby. A great deal of rock had been removed from it and deposited just outside the opening.

An examination of the mine showed that several yards deep into the shaft a portion of it had been closed off with large rocks, presumably from a dynamite blast. It appeared to have been sealed on purpose, but for what reason they could not discern unless it was to keep others from entering.

It has been hypothesized that the Mexicans did not harvest all of the gold out of the shaft and that they sealed it off to protect what was left for the next time they came to the region. As far as anyone knows, they never returned, and whatever was hidden behind the barricade of rocks in the old mine shaft remains a mystery.

15.

Lost Silver of Kings River

Many people believe that the Ozark Mountains were devoid of Indian populations prior to the arrival of the Cherokee, Choctaw, and other tribes during the removal process initiated by the United States government during the 1830s. During this time, Indians were forced out of their homelands in Georgia, the Carolinas, Florida, and Tennessee and relocated in Indian Territory (now Oklahoma), a journey known to history as the Trail of Tears. Some are convinced that the majority of the Indians that inhabited the Ozarks arrived during that time. Nothing could be further from the truth.

The fact is, most of Arkansas, in particular the northwestern section comprising the Ozarks, was home to several tribes that lived peacefully until the arrival of white settlers. Long before the Trail of Tears, a number of Cherokees migrated westward and established settlements in the Ozark Mountains of Arkansas. In addition, the Osage Indians moved in and out of the Ozarks, often remaining for long periods of time if the hunting and fishing were good.

These Indians planted and harvested corn, beans, squash, and other vegetables in the fertile floodplains adjoining streams, large and small, found in the area. In addition, where decent grazing could be obtained, they raised horses and, occasionally, cattle. When the first white men arrived in the Ozark Mountains, they were surprised to find a number of efficient farms operated by the Indian tribes that resided there.

Because game abounded in the forests and fish in the streams, the Indians supplemented agriculture with hunting and fishing. In Carroll County, Arkansas, the King's River was fundamental to the good living found there by the Indians. The King's River flowed northward into Missouri from its spring-fed origin out of the Ozarks' Madison County. So rich and bountiful was the region that when the first white settlers arrived, the Indians welcomed them, shared their bounty with them, and assisted them in starting their own farming and ranching enterprises.

One of the first white men to arrive in this region was Jasper Combs. Combs and his family came to the region in 1820 and developed a small farmstead along the floodplain on one side of the King's River. He grew a few crops and raised some livestock, mostly pigs he had brought with him along the route he traveled from his home in Alabama.

Combs was a friendly and congenial man and got along well with the local Indians. Combs and the Indians often traded farm produce, and on occasion he would invite members of the tribes to his modest cabin to share a meal. Combs and the Indians worked together constructing barns, plowing fields, and hunting. Combs's children played with the Indian young, and in general life in that small valley was good for all.

During many of his dealings with the local Indians, Combs noted that some of them wore armbands and necklaces that appeared to be made from silver. Whenever he inquired about the origin of the metal, which he did from time to time, the Indians would deftly steer the conversation to another topic. Once, when taking a meal at the cabin of an Indian family, Combs observed that several of the cooking utensils were also made from silver. Over time, Combs realized that the Indians did not care to discuss the subject of the metal, so he avoided it. His interest, however, grew keener.

One afternoon, as Combs was gathering sassafras in the woods, he encountered a party of Indians returning from a hunting trip. The men built a small fire and sat around it, talking and discussing the hunt. Combs noted that each of the Indians wore silver ornaments. When he commented on the workmanship evident in the pieces, the Indians said they had fashioned the items themselves from silver they dug from their mine. Seizing the opportunity to learn more, Combs asked them about the mine.

The oldest man in the hunting party told Combs that the silver was dug from a location known only to certain members of the tribe and that it was a carefully guarded secret. To reveal it, he said, meant a swift and certain death at the hands of tribal members. He also claimed that the mine was so well concealed that a person could stand within a few feet of the entrance and not be able to detect it. Knowing how the Indians respected such traditions, and placing significant value on his friendship with these men, Combs dropped the subject.

The 1830s arrived, and with it came the removal of thousands of Indians from their traditional homelands in the southeastern United States. Like the Indians in the Ozarks, members of the Cherokee, Choctaw, Chickasaw, Creek, and Seminole Indian nations had also developed fine and productive farms and settlements, all coveted by white men and politicians. War was waged, and the Indians, outnumbered and out-armed, suffered the consequences and had little choice but to agree to the large-scale removal from their lands. Their forced destination was hundreds of miles to the west, a place designated as Indian Territory. Years later, it would come to be known as Oklahoma. The route along which the evicted tribes were marched is known today as the Trail of Tears.

During the removal process, the United States government also targeted many of the Indians they found in the Ozark Mountains. Most of the Indians living in the King's River Valley were rounded up and escorted out of the area at gunpoint by a military contingent. Before leaving, the Indians negotiated an arrangement with the government to be allowed to maintain ownership of a small parcel of land in their name and that they be allowed to return to it from time to time. The Indians claimed it was a sacred place and served as the burial ground of their ancestors. With reluctance, the government agreed to the proposition. Jasper Combs, however, was convinced that the parcel of land held in trust for the Indians was, in fact, the location of their secret silver mine.

Many years later, Jesse Combs, one of Jasper's sons, recalled the times when the Indians made their annual journey from their reservation in Oklahoma back to the King's River Valley. Arriving in horse-drawn wagons, they would always stop at the Combs residence long enough to visit their old friends. Jasper Combs allowed the Indians to camp on his property while they awaited the arrival of more members of the tribe. Mrs. Combs would prepare meals of venison and pork along with harvests from the garden. Young Jesse Combs said the Indians would remain encamped at this location while they visited their sacred ground. When it was time for them to return to Indian Territory, they drove their wagons out of the valley, each of them loaded down and covered with animal hides.

According to Jesse Combs, the Indians arrived in the valley at least once each year until the onset of the Civil War. As a result of the hostile presence of both Union and Confederate soldiers throughout the Ozark Mountains, the Indians stayed away. By the time the war was over, the tribe had ceased coming to the valley altogether.

Lester Combs was Jesse's son and Jasper's grandson. As a young man, Lester decided to leave the valley and seek his fortune elsewhere. He landed in the town of Springdale, several miles to the west of the King's River Valley, where he held down a job and raised a family. Lester once related a story he heard from his father.

Lester claimed that Jesse Combs met a young Indian while working in a sawmill in the small town of Kingston, located a few miles from the Combs homestead. The Indian youth was familiar with the parcel of land in the river valley that his tribe visited for many years. He told Jesse Combs that his grandfather knew the location of the Indians' secret silver mine. The grandfather, at that time quite elderly, lived on a reservation in Oklahoma.

Jesse Combs, like his father, was intrigued with the notion that valuable silver could be found not far from the family homestead. During the ensuing weeks, Jesse and the young Indian made arrangements for the old man to be brought to the King's River Valley.

When the grandfather arrived, Combs and the young Indian took him to the land that was designated as the Indian allotment. The elder pointed out a number of landmarks he remembered when he had come here as a younger man some sixty years earlier. As the three men walked through the woods, the grandfather reminisced about people, places, and events he recalled from long ago.

After listening to the elder relate his memories for two hours, Jesse Combs asked him what he knew about the location of the silver mine. The grandfather faced Combs and told him that, as a young boy, he had crawled on his hands and knees deep into the shaft to dig out the silver. He said it was a long way from the entrance to the rich vein at the end of the tunnel.

The old man also told Combs about the penalty for revealing the location of the Indians' source of the silver. He hesitated many times during the discussion and made references to the notion that they should leave. Combs persisted, and finally the grandfather said that maybe times had changed and that it might be wise and prudent for the wealth to be used for the good of everyone. He agreed to lead Combs to the mine.

The elder did not locate the mine that day— or the next, or the next. For several weeks, he led Combs and the young Indian throughout a section of the deep forest in the river valley. Along the way, they encountered a number of carvings and signs on rocks and trees, all symbols, explained the old man, that were used by the tribe as directional indicators. Now and then the grandfather would pause and point out a familiar landmark and state that they must be close to the mine, but the day would end without success. In time, he confessed to being confused and lost. He also stated that the mine was hidden so well that no white man could ever find it.

Combs grew impatient and pleaded with the Indian to try to remember, but the old man was tired and finally gave up. He begged for the young Indian to help him return to the reservation in Oklahoma. The next day, the two departed, and it was the last Jesse Combs saw of the old man.

At first, Combs suspected that the grandfather was reluctant to reveal the location of the secret mine because he feared the punishment that he would receive from his tribe. Eventually, he came to believe that the old man just could not remember.

During the next two decades, Jesse Combs explored throughout the woods in the King's River Valley in search of the lost mine, but he was never successful. That the Indians gleaned silver from a large deposit located somewhere in the area was never in question, for members of the Combs family had seen evidence of the ore many times in the form of jewelry, ornaments, utensils, and nuggets.

This much is known. The mine is located in the King's River Valley on a parcel of land that was provided to the tribe that lived there. The boundaries of this parcel of land can be discerned from extant records. Finding the entrance to this mine will likely be the most difficult part of the search. According to what Jesse Combs said, the opening to the shaft was so small that an Indian had to get down on his hands and knees to enter it. Such an opening would be easy to conceal. Members of the Combs family were convinced that the Indians hid the entrance by pushing a large rock across the front of it. They also suspected it was at least partially concealed by natural vegetation such as trees and brush.

It is hidden, to be sure, but it is there. Perhaps some of the older living members of the Indian tribe still know the location. If so, they hold the key to the location of a great fortune in silver ore in the King's River Valley of the Ozark Mountains.

16.

Civil War Artifacts at Mud Creek Bottom

On March 23, 1864, ten thousand Union cavalrymen and foot soldiers departed the garrison at Little Rock, Arkansas and set out toward the south. The force included twelve thousand horses and mules and an estimated one thousand wagons. In addition to provisions and supplies, the wagons transported thousands of rifles along with crates of ammunition.

This large Yankee force was commanded by General Frederick Steele. Steele had orders to rendezvous with the army of General Banks two hundred miles away in Shreveport, Louisiana. There, the two leaders would make preparations for an invasion of selected locations in Texas, the so-called Red River Campaign. Along the way, Steele's troopers were instructed to be on the lookout for Rebel soldiers. If any were found, they were to be confronted and routed. Given the military intelligence reports provided to Steele, he anticipated little to no resistance during the southward trek.

Steele's information proved to be false. Assuming his men would encounter no enemy troops led to a level of overconfidence that resulted in a lack of preparation. This would come back to haunt the general in the form of a disastrous and embarrassing campaign thirty-eight days later when his command limped back into Little Rock.

Underestimating the enemy would turn out to be the cause of failure on several fronts: the Union Army's goals were not met; a significant percentage of the Union force was killed; the Red River Campaign was first disrupted and then abandoned; and wagonloads of materials, including important weaponry, were lost, never to be recovered.

As the column forged its way from Little Rock into southwest Arkansas, they encountered resistance around almost every bend in the road. Skirmishes with the dogged and determined Confederates occurred at Elkins Ford, Hollywood, Okolona, Prairie D'Ane, and Terre Noir Creek. The large numbers of troops associated with the Yankee force yielded what historians have described as victories during these confrontations, but these came at a great cost in human casualties. In spite of these obstacles, they continued on, another poor decision on Steele's part because they experienced further enemy encounters and two dramatic defeats at Marks' Mill and Poison Spring. By this time, Steele's soldiers were in disarray, and the only logical solution was to retreat. Steele ordered the column back to Little Rock.

Steele's army was constantly harassed during its return, with the final battle taking place at Jenkins Ferry, located on the south bank of the Saline River in Grant County. The weary and depleted soldiers were still fifty miles from Little Rock. Though they vastly outnumbered the Confederates, the Yankees were so dispirited and exhausted that all they could think of was returning to the safety of the garrison at Little Rock. The Rebels had shown such unexpected determination through continuous confrontations that Steele had

had to abandon his plan and get his men out of harm's way. Further, they were running out of food for both men and animals.

A major obstacle to returning to Little Rock was due to recent rains that had caused the flooding of the Saline River and adjacent river bottoms. It was estimated that the combined width of the Saline River and the inundated swamps was four miles. The Union soldiers overcame part of the difficulty by constructing a pontoon bridge that spanned the main river channel.

As Yankee soldiers began to move men, horses, and equipment across the bridge, the Confederates attacked from the rear with renewed vigor. History records this as the Battle of Jenkins Ferry, a site that today is a state park. Holding the Rebels at bay, the Union troops managed to cross the river—but not without significant losses of men and animals. Once the entire force had crossed to the other side, Steele ordered the destruction of the pontoon bridge to discourage pursuit.

Steele's troubles were not over. After crossing the river, the army was now forced to make its way through the flooded swamp, an ordeal that further exhausted the already drained soldiers and their travel-weary mounts. After hours of slogging through the muck and mire of the swamp, they arrived at a point where the Little Rock and Pine Bluff roads intersected. Here, Steele ordered a camp to be set up on the nearest high ground and posted a double guard. Fearing that the Confederates might find a way to follow him across the swollen Saline River and swamp, Steele ordered his men awake at four A.M. the next morning and once again set out for Little Rock.

Their route soon took them to a location known as Mud Creek Bottoms, two miles north of their campground of the previous evening. The bottoms, knee- to hip-deep in dark murky water, were five miles long and two miles wide. According to historian Edwin Bearss, the soldiers regarded Mud Creek Bottoms as far more difficult to traverse than the Saline River swamp.

At this point, Steele ordered a contingent of cavalrymen under the leadership of Colonel Carr to take two hundred wagons and press forward with haste to the garrison at Little Rock, procure food, and return to his hungry army as soon as possible. Carr sought a route around the west end of the bottoms. On arriving at a place called Whitmore's Mill, Carr's force encountered a small party of Confederate cavalry. Taken by surprise, Carr's troopers proved to be unprepared and disorganized. Panicking after the first fusillade from the Rebels, they broke ranks and fled northward. Before departing, however, Carr ordered many of the wagons burned so they wouldn't fall into the hands of the Rebels. Long after the war, one could find the remains of these wagons, along with mess kits, military buttons and buckles, artillery shells, and more near the old site of Whitmore's Mill.

Steele led the remainder of his army at a much slower pace than the one assumed by Carr. Passing Whitmore's Mill without incident, Steele continued on for another two miles until coming to Mud Creek. This low area through which the creek flowed proved to be a more intimidating morass of swamp than previously encountered. It was five miles long and four miles wide and called Mud Creek Bottoms.

Hoping to save time, Steele, throwing logic and caution to the wind, led his army into the swamp. The column stretched out for three miles as it snaked through the mud and mire of the boggy environment. The mules pulling the wagons had a difficult time plodding through the deep mud, often sinking into the soft bottom and drowning. Wagons became mired, and many of them had to be abandoned. Before leaving them, Steele had his men set them afire. As the wagons burned, their contents—rifles, ammunition, equipment including cooking pots, canteens, cannonballs, and more—sank into the dark waters and mud of the swamp, where they remain today.

Steele and his men eventually made it back to Little Rock, his army depleted and embarrassed. Along their route, particularly in Mud Creek Bottoms, they had abandoned a wealth of armament and gear. Regarding an attempt at reaching and recovering such items as hopeless, the Union Army never organized any such expedition. The incident was reported, filed, and, in time, forgotten.

Today, a fortune in Union army weaponry and related military gear still lies in Mud Creek Bottoms. Once historical research and publication revealed information of Steele's retreat and abandonment of at least a hundred wagons, treasure and artifact hunters journeyed to Mud Creek Bottoms to try to locate and retrieve some of the contents. It has been estimated that Civil War vintage rifles such as were lost during the flight of Steele's command could bring collector prices of more than $2,000 apiece. Information found in U.S. Army files indicated at least one thousand rifles might have been abandoned in the bottoms.

While Mud Creek Bottoms quickly and easily embraced the trapped wagons, never releasing them, they also provided formidable obstacles to those who would search for its Civil War treasures. The soft muddy bottom is difficult to operate in, often exhausting the hardiest of adventurers who enter this region. Patches of quicksand must be contended with, and if that were not enough, the treasure hunter may encounter rattlesnakes, water moccasins, copperheads, ticks, and leeches. Large snapping turtles lurking in the

Stygian waters have occasionally interfered with the activities of those who would enter the area in search of treasure. Other bottoms in this part of Arkansas have dried up during drought periods, thus allowing entry for timber cutters and sportsmen. The spring-fed Mud Creek Bottoms, however, have always maintained their water level.

Today, a logging road runs through Mud Creek Bottoms, an elevated gravel route that transects the swamp. In the area, dozens of minié balls and other Civil War artifacts have been found, apparently churned up from the bottom muck during road construction. Even more significantly, the remains of a Civil War-era wagon have been found at a point where the road intersects a small creek deep in the swamp.

It is a small leap of faith to consider that only a few inches or feet below the surface of the dark waters of Mud Creek Bottoms lies a fortune in Civil War Union Army rifles and other artifacts. Thus far, the watery environment, along with its denizens, has proven to be an effective barrier to recovery.

Selected Bibliography

Books and Articles

Allsopp, Fred W. *Folklore of Romantic Arkansas, Volume I*. The Grolier Society, 1931.

Arkansas Gazette. "Treasure Hunters May Seek Fabled Gold." September 18, 1976.

Bowers, Rodney. "Looking for Lost Spanish Mine." *Arkansas Gazette*, September 25, 1988.

Curlee, Mabel. "Hidden Treasure." *Baxter County History* 3.3: 44–46, n.d.

Dickason, Doris. "Gold Diggin's at Golden City." *Wagon Wheels* 2.4: 18–19, n.d.

Garland, Russell L. *Immigrants in the Ozarks*. Columbia: University of Missouri Press, 1939.

Jameson, W.C. *Buried Treasures of the American Southwest*. Little Rock: August House, Inc., 1989.

———. *Buried Treasures of the Ozarks*. Little Rock: August House, Inc., 1990.

———. "Inn at Happy Bend." *True West* 31.6 (January 1984): 29–30.

———. "The Legend of Golden City." *True West* 35.4 (April 1988): 26–29.

———. "The Legend of the Lost Soldier's Bluff." *The Arkansawyer* 1.4 (March–April 1985): 22–23

———. "The Lost Cossatot Gold Mine." *Arkansas Times* 14.10 (June 1988): 23–26.

———. *Lost Mines and Buried Treasures of Arkansas*. Hendersonville, Tennessee: Goldminds Publishing, 2011.

———. "Lost Treasure of the Cossatot." *True West* 31.10 (January 1985): 47–49.

———. "Tobe Inmon's Silver Bullets." *True West* 33.3 (March 1986): 60–61.

Kelley, J. C. "Aged Settler Recalls Rush to Golden City." *Booneville Democrat*, 1929 (date unknown).

Lambrecht, Gordon. "Gold." *Baxter County History* 1.4: 51, n.d.

McCartney, Scott. "Treasure Tales Prove Puzzling." *Arkansas Democrat*, April 26, 1987.

Page, Tate C. *The Voices of Moccasin Creek*. Point Lookout, Missouri: School of the Ozarks Press, 1972.

Rafferty, Milton D. *The Ozarks: Land and Life*. Norman: University of Oklahoma Press, 1980.

Roberts, Jim. "Golden City, Arkansas." *Booneville Democrat*, April 1946.

Steele, Phillip. *Lost Treasures of the Ozarks*. Springdale, Arkansas: privately published, n.d.

Tatham, Robert L. *Ozark Treasure Tales*. Ragtown, Missouri: R. L. Tatham Company, 1979.

Interviews

Driftwood, Jimmy. Timbo, Arkansas, March 7, 1983.

Grinder, Doyle. Marshall, Arkansas, June 1982.

Grinder, Erna Mae. Marshall, Arkansas, June 1982.

Page, Tate C. Russellville, Arkansas, July 2, 1981.